# Capitol Offenses
## House For Sale

by Joe Randazzo

A Sprezzatura Book
from New Renaissance Press

Sprezzatura Books
New Renaissance Press
8 Woodside Drive
South Burlington, VT 05403

**ISBN  978-0-9851615-2-1**

**Library of Congress Control Number
2015905947**

This book is a work of fiction. Character names and incidents in the plot are products of the author's imagination. Any resemblance to actual events or persons, living or dead, is entirely coincidental.

Author's photograph: Chris Valentine
Cover photographs courtesy of Shutterstock

For Rita Randazzo, Such a Lovely Woman

Also by Joe Randazzo

**Poetry**
*Coffee House*
*His/Hers: Mars and Venus Write Poetry*
(with Rita Randazzo)

**Novels**
*Screen*
*Van Eyck's Secret*
*See Dick Run: A Grownup's Picture Book*
*Walking Man*
*Afterworld*
*The Strange Metamorphosis of Zachary Warren*

**Photodocumentary**
*Going With the Wind: Carolina In My Mind*

Advance Comments for *Capitol Offenses*

Nick Hades understands power.  He has a great appreciation for the simple fact that the weak are not supposed to survive.  Howard Roark would approve.

Ayn Rand

Hades knows that corruption is a part of a grand order.  When you disagree with Nick Hades, you can wind up dead.

Boss Tweed

Did you ever notice that people with no money always criticize those who have made it big?  Hades is one of us.  He is an honorary baron.  When he passes on to the Afterworld, I'll be his mentor down here.

Cornelius Vanderbilt

Do you know what a liberal is?  A liberal is a conservative who has no knowledge of the real world.  He is an immature, untested theorist who will cry foul when life interrupts his stupid dreams.  Nick Hades has the thankless job of re-indoctrinating these commie sissies so they can function as real Americans.

Joe McCarthy

There is nothing to fear but people like Nick Hades.

Franklin D. Roosevelt

Hades did what I should have done.  I should have denied any wrongdoing and blamed it on jealous Democrats.  Republicans everywhere can learn a great deal from this man.

Richard Nixon

Nick Hades is the enemy of every thinking woman.

Susan B. Anthony

# 1

"**M**r. President!   Mr. President!"

"Yes, John?"

"Thank you, Mr. President.   How would you comment, sir, on Vladimir Putin's allegation that the United States and Saudi Arabia are deliberately lowering oil prices to ruin the Russian economy?"

"Good question.  As past speaker of the house, I have observed the Russian premier for several years, and I have come to the conclusion that he has absolutely no sense of humor."

"Mr. President?"

"Yes, Nancy."

"Now that you and the first family have moved into the White House, are Alfonso and Petunia going to be allowed to keep their pets?  I like the way Alfonso pulls the doggies' ears.  Their yelps and growls are so cute."

"Well, Nancy, that is a bone of contention in our family, no pun intended.  The White House is full of antique treasures, and having four uber-killer Rottweilers is not a good idea.  So, I donated them to the Capitol Police.  I bought the kids other pets."

"What pets are those, Mr. President?"

"Gerbils. They each have two gerbils in large, very ornate gilt cages. They can watch them live their daily lives, you know, spinning on those little yellow wheels, screwing happily away in the open. The first gerbils will teach them a lot about life. Much better than watching *Dancing with the Degenerates*. They never really *do* anything to each other in front of all those lights and cameras."

"Mr. President?"

"Yes, the colored man in the back row."

President Hades turns to his assistant and asks her to scan the identity badge of the reporter who wants to be acknowledged. Rhoda Dendron points the laser reader at his badge and reports to the president. She whispers in his ear.

"His name is Chandu Gupta, and he's from *New Delhi Times*."

"I am sorry, sir, we are taking questions only from American reporters at this time. I will have another briefing for alternate types like you in a week or two."

"Mr. President?"

"Yes, the tall, dark-haired woman with the first three buttons of her blouse unbuttoned."

"Thank you, Mr. President. My name is Fanny Mucha. What do you feel your greatest challenge will be once you get settled into your new living environment? Will it be creating jobs and other domestic items, or will it be to revamp and streamline our foreign policy?"

"Excellent, Miss Mucha! Rarely do questions contain their own answers. Revamp and streamline indeed. Speaking of being streamlined, you must tell me more of your ideas in private. Next question…the man in the third row who is waving his arms wildly. I do not want you to sustain a separated shoulder, for government insurance reasons. Rhoda, please scan his identity badge."

She quietly whispers, "Mr. President, his name is Harvey Schwartz, and he's from the *New York Times*. He's an American citizen, but according to historical data was involved in the Occupy Movement several years ago. He was detained by the New York Police and is considered the most left-wing reporter on their staff."

"Thank you, Rhoda. What is your question, Mr. Schwartz?"

"Mr. President, why don't you have any women or people of color on your cabinet?"

"Mr. Schwartz, you are Jewish, are you not? Well, when you go to your favorite discount store to buy furniture at what I am sure will be the lowest possible price, you can choose whatever cabinet you like. I will choose mine without owing liberals like you an explanation."

"How dare you, Mr. President! You're unfairly typecasting me, and that's an anti-Semitic statement."

"Security, please remove Mr. Schwartz from the briefing room. I will not tolerate dissent that only serves to further the specific agenda of the questioner. If any of you have a particular axe to grind, you had better go elsewhere. In my administration, we will pursue the only grand truth, the American Truth. I will take another question. Yes, the woman in the fourth row who keeps crossing and uncrossing her legs to expose her green lace underwear."

"Thank you, Mr. President. My name is Foxxy Hart. Isn't it a bit unusual for an incoming president to not have chosen his chief of staff, his press secretary, or to name his secretaries of State, Treasury, and the Department of Defense? What are you waiting for, sir? Is there some reason why you haven't made these choices? Some people may think that you have trouble making decisions."

"Miss Hart, when those decisions are finally made, you will be the first to know. I will give you an exclusive interview. I will make my decision on the basis of how they all work together. In the past, presidents have picked their staff based solely on individual qualifications. To me, the team concept is everything. How will we all interact in a small, hot room, when the chips are down, when everyone is tired, drinking too much, the pizza is cold and stale, someone just farted, and the fate of our Republic hangs in the balance? In the days ahead, those are the kind of leaders I will surround myself with."

"Mr. President."

"Yes, the man in the third row with the nervous tic."

"Thank you, Mr. President. When you looked at your *go, go, go,* gold Rolex watch a few moments ago, I thought I saw a *ta, ta, ta,* tattoo on your left arm. Did you recently get a tattoo?"

"Oh, that." The president looks skyward.   Nora Hades giggles.

"Mr. President, why did you get a tattoo?" Myra Glock, a female reporter from the *Washington Post,* energetically interrupts.

"I can see this will not go away until I explain myself.  As you know, we were in Indonesia for an extended vacation three weeks ago.  While we were there we went to...what was that city again, Hon?"  The President turns to Nora, who answers quietly.

"Right, it was in Labuan Bajo.  We were celebrating our election victory, a total sweep over the Democrats in all houses, and we were slightly under the weather, if you know what I mean.  We sort of drifted into this dark den with thick smoke in the air and cushions all over the floor, and it seemed like a good idea at the time."

"What kind of tattoo is it?" Myra Glock again raises her voice.

"Miss Glock, it is a tattoo of a dragon.  It starts just above my wrist on both arms, goes around my body, across both the front and the back, missing no significant areas."

"Why did you choose a dragon, Mr. President?"

"When I was little, I saw this great Disney cartoon about a pet Komodo Dragon.  It really moved me, and I have loved dragons ever since.  That is why we vacationed in Indonesia."

"What cartoon was that, sir? Aren't Komodo Dragons poisonous man-eaters?"

"I do not remember the name of the cartoon. Snakes are also supposed to be poisonous, but I allowed you in here just the same, Miss Glock. Next question. Yes, the short, olive-skinned man right here in the first row. Are you also a foreign correspondent? One moment, sir. Rhoda, please scan his badge."

"His name is Sal DiPalma, and he's from the *Philadelphia Enquirer*. He's third generation Italian-American and served in both Iraq and Afghanistan. He's also a member of the NRA and teaches courses in self-defense."

"Excellent! Thank you, Rhoda. Before you ask your question, Mr. DiPalma, let me just say that you are the perfect example of everything that is right with America. In you I see the evolution of a true American. In spite of your southern European roots, your dark-olive skin is getting lighter with each generation, as your family intermarries with Scots-Irish and other Nordic strains. In sixty to seventy years, no one who looks at your grandchildren will be able to determine the place your ancestors came from, and I guarantee they will not be denied membership in any clubs that are now shutting you out. I find your unwritten and unspoken story very moving and uplifting. One of my Herculean tasks as your new president will be to achieve the right color balance. Immigration is an important issue. White birth rates are declining. Hispanics and EyeTalians are sneaking into this country under the barbed wire and across the mine fields, and our overall hue has darkened in the last few generations. I intend to reverse that trend.

"Actually, we are out of time. Thank you, ladies and gentlemen."

# 2

**D**ear MoveOver Member:

We hope you will join the Independent Senator from Vermont in her quest for political justice, and to end once and for all the undue influence that PAC money has on our electoral process.

Greetings Everyone,

I'm Bernice Sandcastle from Vermont. One month ago President Hades took office. The Krotch brothers, Karl and Adolph, contributed 970 million dollars to Republican candidates. It's no secret that it was this huge influx of money that helped defeat all the Democrats who ran in hotly contested races. It seems the American people can't make the right decision when they view hate ads that appear before or after beer commercials during football games. Whatever they see, they automatically accept as gospel truth.

The University of Vermont's polling service says that the last election was decided during the Super Bowl game, between the third and fourth quarters. That's when Krotch PAC-funded ads alleged that Democratic candidates never attended football games, owned rifles, or drove in pickup trucks. The Republican National Committee used Krotch money to skillfully place 50 different ads, one in each state, to target the senators, representatives, and governors who were, in their words, 'standing in the way of American greatness.' At the end of every one of these spots, President Hades was shown driving in his shiny-new red pickup truck, with a gold cross hanging from his rearview mirror, his slavering Rotweillers riding in the back, his AR15 rifle hung on two hooks over the rear window of the cab, and sitting next to him, some big-breasted blonde in a tight white sweater who he picked up at the quick-stop an hour earlier.

We've got to break the stranglehold the Krotch brothers have on American politics. As a reward for his immense contribution, Adolph Krotch has been named to head the Securities and Exchange Commission and is now in charge of regulating Wall Street. This is like putting your home mortgage in Bernie Madoff's bank account. What's next, will we be arrested for not investing in Wall Street? I hate to use fear as a tactic to motivate people, but there you have it. The only thing the Krotch brothers and the Republican party love and respect is money. Even more than power or fame, it's money that drives them.

Let's fight back! I want each of you to hit them where it really hurts, in their Krotch pockets. Let's shut them down by not buying any of their products or having anything to do with the organizations they sponsor or support. Won't you join me in turning America around?

Stay away from:

General Foods
Kraft Foods
Kellogg Corporation
Post Cereals
Westinghouse

General Electric
Sears
Vegetables
Fruit
Target
Costco
Piggly Wiggly
Monsanto
Lockheed Martin
Iowa
Sony
Samsung
General Motors
Ford
Chrysler
Toyota
Honda
Belgium
Dell Computers
China
Santa Monica
San Diego
San Francisco
California
Florida
Verizon
Amazon
Black Boots
Indiana
Dancing With the Degenerates
Wheel of Fortune
Supermarkets
Texas

Hardware Stores
Veterinarians
Pfizer
Viagra
Google
Microsoft
Alfalfa
Soy
Corn
Ice Cream
Shoes
Gasoline
Heating Oil
Air
Water
The United States Government
and Ted Nugent


Thank you,

*Bernice Sandcastle*

United States Senator – Vermont




MoveOver.orgy is sponsoring a mass call-a-thon.  We're going to call all the corporations and other entities on Senator Sandcastle's list and tell them how much we hate them. Won't you sign up to host a house party next weekend?

Thanks for all that you do.

Jaime, Henrietta, Percival K., Minerva, and the rest of the team

Help build the momentum—start a monthly donation ***here*** or chip in a one-time donation ***here***.

---

# 3

"Hello, Foxxy. Please sit down. I promised you an exclusive when I decided on my staff picks. Oh, I just saw your knickers! Instead of green, they are now purple. Of course you may use your recorder. I have nothing to hide. However, please erase that comment about your knickers. I do not want citizens to get the wrong idea.

"As you already know, Adolph Krotch is in charge of the SEC. He is doing great. He just wrote an article for the *Wall Street Journal* entitled, 'The Hidden Joys of Insider Trading.' I know a reformer when I see one.

"Karl Krotch is my pick for secretary of the Interior. Who knows the inner workings of America better than he does? He now owns most of our newspapers and cable stations. It does not matter what the facts are, he will simply rearrange them.

"Rhoda Dendron is my choice for press secretary and chief of staff. Shit, she already does everything else, if you know what I mean. If I do not give her a title, she could make trouble. She knows too much about my....erm....cabinet and computer systems.

"Dwayne Lapoopierre for the ATF. I love his plan to bring back fully automatic suppressed weapons for the average American. If a person does not have a criminal record, why should he not be permitted to own a machine gun with a silencer? I want the world to know that not only does America *have* an army, America *is* an army.

"Sarah Lapin for the American Association for the Advancement of Science (AAAS). Now we are off the record, do you understand? I am afraid this is a bit of manipulation on my part. You see, I view science, especially the cockamamie theories on global warming, as a direct threat to my administration. Fortunately for us, Sarah does not understand scientific theory. As a matter of fact, she does not understand basic arithmetic. By the time she is finished chairing the association, she will set experimentation and discovery back three decades. Yup, she is perfect.

"Jboo Boehnhead has been reconfirmed as Speaker of the House. He is a team player. In other words, he will do exactly what I tell him to. It is either that or I will expose what he did at last year's Christmas party.

"Itch McCringell is now the Majority Leader in the Senate. He has good instincts, but he sometimes forgets that the money he siphons off must not *all* go into his pocket. He needs a reminder now and then to fill mine. All I have to do is call him into the Oval Office and drag out that photograph. He becomes Silly Putty afterwards. Too bad his wife is such a dog, because at that moment I could have my way...Oh, never mind.

"Ludwig Peckeroff from Oklahoma is my choice for Secretary of State. He knows how to use a shotgun. He always travels with two cases of semi-automatic 12-gauges. When he unloads them from his State Department plane, no towelhead is going to give him any shit. The era of touchy-feely Democratic statesmanship is at a joyous end. The only way to not get beat up by a bully is to be a tougher bully. Teddy knew that. We once had a great Republican vice president who knew how to shoot a shotgun, even if his aim was a bit low.

"My Secretary of the Treasury is also the CEO of The Bank of American Commerce, Coin Goldman. I decided it will be a lot easier to combine the assets of our Treasury with the largest sub-prime lender in American history. There will be no more wheeling and dealing, trying to finagle an untidy profit here and there. Now all the money will all be under one roof and funds can be siphoned off with impunity. Look at these new hundred-dollar bills with my photograph replacing that of Ben Franklin. That picture of me was taken the year I graduated with a law degree from the University of Indiana. This is history, Foxxy! Never before has a sitting American president had his portrait on paper money of any denomination. The Democrats tried, but we weren't printing three-dollar bills at the time, har har, hardy har har!

"Do not forget, there is bound to be at least one, and possibly two, openings on the Supreme Court during my term. Antibody Scalia, Clarabell Thomas and Sameold Alito have been good friends to the Republican Party. As you know, my wife Nora is also an attorney. I will consult with her on who she recommends to fill the upcoming vacancies. This is another first, Foxxy! Make sure you write about it. I do not pay lip service to giving women a voice in my government. My wife will decide the nominees, even if she doesn't have a title or specific recognized power, and sheeple will think it came from me.

"What was the question, Foxxy? Will she choose herself? Oh, hell no. Can you see that hot little number dressed in a black robe, sitting next to those antiques discussing God knows what-all? Not a chance. I am sure she has something much bigger in mind for herself.

"For Secretary of Defense I choose Lance Corporal Dirk Groggin of the United States Marine Corps. Corporal Groggin registered the most sniper kills in Iraq, Afghanistan, and along our Mexican border, 837 to be exact. Who would you rather have controlling our military, some she/he who has never fired a gun, or the best in the business?

"I will not choose heads for the Environmental Protection Agency, the Food and Drug Administration, the National Endowment of the Arts, or the Social Security Administration. For the time being, their directors will remain in place. We will discuss those agencies at another meeting.

"So, Foxxy, timing is important in releasing or leaking information. Your job is to put this stuff out to online and print media. In return you get exclusive information that no one else has. It's a win-win for us both. Our next meeting is at your place, at night. Late at night."

# 4

The White House has 132 rooms, 35 bathrooms, 147 windows, 412 doors, 28 fireplaces, 8 staircases, and 3 elevators arranged over 6 floors. When Nick Hades was governor of Indiana, the family lived in the mansion in Indianapolis, a typical English Tudor home of only 10,500 square feet, 23 rooms, and 11 bathrooms. The family was very excited to leave provincial mid-America behind for the most famous home in the United States.

The first family was given a massive book filled with descriptions and photos of all the furniture suites in the White House inventory. They each got to choose their favorites and to mix and match whatever suited their fancy.

Petunia and Alfonso were especially excited to move into the White House because, according to them, nothing ever happens in Indiana. Now they both have 900-square-foot East Rooms that can easily accommodate their extensive accumulations.

Petunia chose a canopy bed with pink ruffles and edging, and a white, Queen Anne-style dresser, desk, and loveseat. There is gold trim on all the edges, and the tops of the desk and dresser are pure white Carrara marble.

Alfonso chose the same furniture that was used by the Kennedy family. He demanded, however, that the pieces be refinished, or rather re-painted, in his favorite color. The White House archivist tried to explain that early Colonial Chippendale Philadelphia pieces should never be refinished because it destroys their value, but Alfonso whined until he got his way. His bed, dresser, desk, end tables, card table, and sofa are now all painted purple.

Nora told both of them that they could put anything they wanted on their walls as long as it wasn't obscene. She said that guests are often shown the first family's living quarters, and she doesn't want nude photos of their favorite rap stars shocking the public.

Petunia hates being told what to do, so she displayed her favorite three-by-seven-foot photo of a naked Snotty Droopy Dingo Doggy holding an assault rifle, but she cut out a small American flag and pasted it over his most sensitive spot. Nora agreed that it was a good compromise.

Madeleine Soufflé has been the family cook for thirty years, since long before the children were born. She followed them from their original home in Kokomo, to the governor's mansion, and now to the White House. She's fitting in nicely. They immediately gave her a staff of five, and she has full control over all the dishes that are prepared by the other chefs. There is a separate kitchen in the White House that creates nothing but sweets.

However, Nick Hades is a traditionalist when it comes to food. He likes to eat the same things on the same days, day in and day out, week after week. It makes things simple for Ms. Soufflé, at least as far as he's concerned. The rest of the family has never eaten what their father eats, in spite of his constantly trying to interest them in his Sunday ham and artichoke hearts.

Of the many dining rooms, the Hades family chose to eat in the Yellow Room near the Oval Office. It's a small, intimate area with a fireplace and a carved white mantle. They removed "The Peacemakers," an 1868 painting of Abraham Lincoln by George P.A. Healy, and replaced it with a Batman movie poster. There is an ornate chandelier above a large round table that seats four. The display cabinets are full of eighteenth-century cups and vases, and there are elegant green-flowered drapes hung over the ten-foot-tall windows.

Madeleine Soufflé and her staff have prepared the evening meal, and the Hades family has sat down to Sunday dinner. The tablecloth is a fine, hand-crocheted pattern reminiscent of designs found on the Aran Islands in Ireland. The china is a mid-twentieth-century design, manufactured in New York, and has hand-painted scenes from national forests and parks located throughout the fifty states. The sterling silverware is in the 1935 American Beauty pattern, and each person has a special four-inch Petites Reflection tasting spoon alongside the freshly prepared fruit cup to start their meal.

"Stop it, Pizza-Face! Mom, she threw a soggy cherry at me and it landed in my lap."

"Don't talk like that to your sister."

"Cut it out, you dick-brained retard! Mom, he kicked me under the table."

"Don't kick your sister, and don't talk like that to your brother."

"How can you eat ham every Sunday? You're gonna turn into a pig."

"Petunia, don't talk like that to your father."

"Dad, how come the vice president wasn't at your news conference? Did you have him locked up? His breath always smells like mint.  Is he trying to hide something?  It reminds me of the TV show we saw last night, *House of Cards*, only this is a House of Turds. What kind of food is this?  I'm not going to eat this shit!  Where's my hamburger?"

"Alfonso, Vice President Grouse isn't feeling well, and why are you so preoccupied with turds?"

"I'm sorry, Mom, this food is dog cah cah, is that better?  Where's my hamburger?"

"Don't talk like that in front of the servers."

# 5

Senator Jim McCann of North Dakota is Chairman of the Armed Services Committee. As a member of President Hades' cabinet, he was invited to present his plans to implement a brand new presidential Directive. Missing from this first cabinet meeting, and from all other functions, is the vice president. Daniel Grouse has had the flu and a badly sprained ankle. He's been out of the public eye for over a month, ever since the inauguration. At least, that's the *official* word. However, President Hades knows that Grouse has a drinking problem and secretly entered AA to get control of his addiction. The president used one of his aides to smuggle top-quality Scotch into his rehab center. It's in Hades' best interest to keep Grouse drunk and out of his way, until he decides what to do with him. The Republican party put heavy pressure on him to choose Grouse as his running mate. They were right, because without him on the ticket, Hades would never have won the northeast and central swing states. But Grouse is too liberal, much too liberal, for comfort.

The cabinet meeting has a higher purpose for the president. It will show him how his chosen staff will work together. He will see if they are inventive and act on their own without his constant prodding, or require a hands-on leader who must drive even the minutia of each agenda.

The meeting room in the Oval Office has twenty-two chairs. President Hades does not insist that cabinet members turn off their phones and other portable devices. However, he has a projector and amplifier at the center of the table, aimed at a six-by-nine-foot screen at the far end of the room. If anyone gets a call or text message, they must plug in their devices to the amplifier/projector for all to see and hear. As a result, everyone turns off their portables before entering the room. The president is proud of his new rule. He has learned to banish and forbid annoyances, by not actively banishing or forbidding them. If anyone from the press asks him whether or not it was true that he doesn't allow phones and devices during his cabinet meetings, he can deny it and be telling the "truth."

Hades will try to perfect this motivational approach in the months to come. By making rules that do not seem restrictive, he doesn't present the appearance of a dictator. He still gets his way, using a velvet-smooth Fascist style that he learned from the writings of Benito Mussolini.

After the usual introductions and some nervous laughter, Senator McCann takes a drink of spiked apple cider from the cut-glass pitcher and makes his presentation.

"Mr. President and fellow cabinet members, I'm honored to kick off the first item of this new and bold administration. I thank the president for the opportunity to help lead this country out of the cellar and back to our former greatness."

"What have you got for us, Jim?" the president asks.

"As some of you may know, there are people who are upset at our Army recruiting posters that say 'For God and Country.' They claim that it isn't right to kill for God. Of course, we all most ardently disagree with that objection, but it got me to thinking about what else we can offer new recruits. There has been a falloff in the quality of incoming soldiers. We need to get new recruits quickly into what I call Quality Combat Status.

"Here's how we can do it. As you know, the goons in ISIL believe that when they die in battle, they go to their garden of delights to meet all the vestal virgins. What I'm proposing for our boys is a third item in addition to killing for God and country. We should advertise that new recruits can kill for God, country, and some poontang.

"Think about it. If our airborne troops kill people in battle, they get to spend the night with the likes of Sarah Lapin, Michelle Bacchanalia, or Ann Cutlet. It's a win-win for everyone. ISIL soldiers want to die to see their virgins, and we want to kill them to sleep with ours. Unfortunately, I couldn't find any right-wing Republican virgins, but the three people I mentioned aren't afraid of heights and are willing to parachute into the front lines."

"Excellent, Jim!" the president exclaims. "What is the point of proving you are a man if you do not get a chance to enjoy yourself once you have finished fighting for God?"

# 6

**N**ora Hades is concerned that having her family suddenly thrust into the national limelight has put tremendous pressure on them all. Her marriage is showing signs of strain. Nick is staying up late at night looking at pornography while he cleans his guns, and she is fantasizing about two secret agents who are closely guarding them. One is a man and the other is a woman. Petunia snuck out of the White House, eluded her security detail, and went into the seedy part of Washington to buy drugs. Alfonso has been playing violent video games nonstop every night until three in the morning.

In other words, they're acting like a fairly typical American family. Although they go to church, The Church of the Trampoline in South Washington, it's only for show. They each have a small iPod that they smuggled into the service last Sunday to distract themselves from the pastor's sermon on self-sacrifice. They are all very skillful at using their devices while everyone else in the congregation has bowed their heads in prayer. They place the pods in the hymn books and mouth the words while they text their friends.

Although Nick objected, Nora finally persuaded him to let a family counselor visit the White House every Tuesday evening. She was given an open-ended security clearance and is automatically checked through when she presents her badge. As far as his staff is concerned, Dr. Carla Gung is the family biographer. She brings her camera to further the ruse.

It's Tuesday night and the family is gathered in Petunia's room. Dr. Gung chose her room to get the president's daughter more involved in the therapy. However, it was Nora's idea that the doctor is not allowed to speak the words "therapy" or "analysis" to anyone. As far as the children are concerned, Carla is the social director who is in charge of helping the family make a smooth transition into the White House. She is also the family confidant, and anything spoken in private will not leave the White House. She is available to meet with anyone of the four in a special private session if necessary. She is being paid a handsome retainer of $340,000 per year to be on call when and if she is needed, 24/7, 365 days a year. Naturally, both Petunia and Alfonso know that she's a shrink, and they're having a wonderful time deciding how they are going to mess with her mind and repay their parents for having to endure the weekly psychobabble.

The first session is for all of them to get acquainted.

"Hello, my name is Carla. You must be Petunia. You're fifteen, and this is Alfonso, twelve years old. Did I get that right? I just know we're going to get along famously. How has your day gone, Alfonso?"

"Wow, I'm really impressed with you, Dr. Carla. You knew that I'm Alfonso. That's a brilliant insight. I think it's really neat, actually awesome, that you got your doctorate in social directing. Was that from the Sam Houston Institute of Technology in Texas, you know, good old SHIT?"

"I think I detect some hostility coming from you, Alfonso. You are Alfonso, aren't you? I hope I didn't offend you by calling you that. You know, there are so many transgendered people out there, I have to be careful. And what about you, Petunia? How did your day go?"

"Don't call me a dago, you kraut!"

"I think I sense some hostility coming from you, Petunia. I also notice what smells like burnt tea coming from your hair. Have you been smoking marijuana?"

"Oh no, Dr. Gung. I have *never* smoked marijuana. I have blown a whole bunch of weed, as we youngsters call it, if that helps in this session. Tell me, doctor, are you married? And how old are you?"

"I'm honored that you take an interest in me. No, I'm not married, and..."

"Are you gay?"

"No, I'm not gay, but I...."

"How old are you?"

"I'm forty-seven, although most people say that I look fifteen years younger. What do you think? Do you think I look my age?"

"Is that important to you, doctor?"

"Yes, absolutely! It's very important to any person, and especially a professional woman, to feel appreciated for both her looks *and* intelligence. Petunia, do you and Alfonso like the way I style my hair, and the way I show a little skin above my knee? Oh nuts, here I go talking about myself. This is supposed to be about you guys. President Hades, what do *you* think of me?"

# 7

**V**ice President Grouse has resigned.  Under intense pressure from President Hades, which included the threat to expose his severe drinking problem, Grouse elected to return to private life and become a lobbyist for HealthMax Pharmaceuticals.  In a bold move, the president decided that the two finalists for his replacement would debate in front of the American people to make a convincing case why they should be chosen.  Although the final decision must be his alone, this debate will give Hades a good idea how the future vice president will perform in crisis mode.

They are both conservatives.  One is a woman, Senator Jan McDrewer from Nevada.  The other is Percy Floy, congressman from the 28th district of Iowa.  Hades is looking ahead to the next election.  He thinks a woman on the ticket might get minority votes that could otherwise go to the Democratic candidate.  However, deep down inside, he despises the idea of having his photo with Jan McDrewer on campaign buttons, bumper stickers, placard posters, and other media mailings.  At one time Jan was hot, but now Father Time has dropped what needs to be upright.

"Good evening, ladies and gentlemen.  I'm Jim Trapezoid.  Welcome to the vice presidential debate between Senator Jan McDrewer from Nevada and Congressman Percy Floy from Iowa.  Each candidate will have three minutes, and the other candidate will have two for rebuttal.  Back and forth repartee will be tolerated.  It will be up to the moderator to cut off discussion on any particular topic.  You will each alternate in speaking first on the questions posed by our panel, the esteemed co-anchors of FLOX News: Hymie Wart, and Bill O'Hara. Before we begin, President Hades would like to say a few words."

"Thank you, Jim, and welcome to our debate. First of all, I would like to thank Daniel Grouse for his service to our country. It takes courage to know when to pack it in, and I admire his leadership. He has proven that he puts his country first.

"American citizens would normally get to see the vice presidential candidates debate *before* the election. I thought it only right to continue that tradition, even if it is after the fact, and I will be solely in charge of the outcome. Now, on to the debate. By a flip of the coin the first question is from Hymie and is for Congressman Floy."

"Thank you, Mr. President. Congressman Floy, the Iowa papers circulated a story last year about your involvement in awarding building contracts to your friends. One of them reportedly bought you a new Cadillac. How would you comment on that?"

"You have to look at the facts, Hymie. As governor and later as congressman from Iowa, I was in charge of, and awarded contracts for, a hundred different projects. I also have hundreds of friends. Doesn't it make bloody good sense that sooner or later one of my friends should happen to back into one of my projects? As for the car, that's what good friends do for each other. It's a non-story, and a major waste of everyone's time."

"Senator McDrewer, you have two minutes for rebuttal."

"That question has never come up in all the years I've been in public office because I never make the final decision on who will do the work. I leave that to the experts in each field. I only signed off on the need for a specific project. The implementation was for others who were once removed from the companies. With me there has never been a conflict of interest."

"Next question is from Bill for Senator McDrewer."

"Senator, on three occasions in the last four years, you voted with the Republicans on immigration reform. Last week it was reported that you have changed your position. How has it changed?"

"Mr. OHara, I have not changed my position. That story was leaked by Congressman Floy's staff. He's the one who hires undocumented aliens for his household. He's the one who allowed the major hospital in his state to go unpunished for refusing treatment for sick illegal children. He's the one who got his Mexican maid pregnant and then threw her out of the house."

"You betcha, Sweetie, and I'd do it again in a heartbeat. Sure, I use aliens to clean the house, that's all they're good for, for Christ's sake. What do you want me to do, grab 'em off the street and put them in charge of the Iowa National Bank?"

"Don't call me Sweetie! I wonder if you're under the influence as we speak? You have a history of womanizing and betraying your wife and family, including that affair with the porn-star twins. If you can't be true to your family, how can the American people count on you to be true to your country?"

"My private life is none of your or anybody else's damn business. When I was seeing those twins I was separated from my wife."

"Oh really, and still living in the same house with your family and the twins. How did you manage that?"

"I think it's time to move on to another question. Hymie has a question for Congressman Floy."

"Congressman, you have come out against legalized marijuana in Washington D.C. Yet the record shows that you had four drug arrests while you were in college, and one for distributing pills while you were a congressional intern. Could you comment, sir?"

"If it's legal for others to buy pot, and get pills from their doctors, it should be legal for me as well. There aren't going to be two sets of rules, one for me, and one for everybody else."

"You're supposed to be a role model. How can you expect others not to use drugs if you have used them yourself?" Senator McDrewer throws up her arms in exasperation.

"Oh, you're so goody-goody. Everyone thinks you're so squeaky clean. We turned up something that will interest the American people. When you were a senior in college you had an affair with your law professor. Is that or is that not true?"

Senator McDrewer begins to speak, but then hesitates and blushes as she stares down at her notes. "He made me feel special. I hero-worshiped him, and he took advantage of me because of his tenured position. It took me another ten years before I was mature enough to have a real relationship."

Fifteen minutes later the debate was over. FLOX news anchor and moderator Jim Trapezoid summed up the debate on his evening news program:

"Congressman Percy Floy of Iowa was selected by the president to be his VP. Floy easily outdebated Senator McDrewer when she admitted, as an unmarried woman, to a capital indiscretion while still a senior in college. There are certain things the American people will not forgive."

# 8

"**W**elcome to the Oval Office. As some of you may know, back in the 1930s, Democratic President Franklin D. Roosevelt spoke to Americans in what were called Fireside Chats. These were radio programs, mostly about his opinions. He liked to speak on the radio because he looked terrible in person, you know, in that wheelchair. Still, it was neat to involve the average American, even if he was trying to brainwash them to his brand of socialism.

"I'm going to start a new tradition. There's no working fireplace in the Oval Office so I can't have a Fireside Chat. Most of you don't have fireplaces either. It makes no sense to have a Fireside Chat for Christ's sake if you live in Palm Beach. So I'm going to call our monthly meetings Significations and Redemptions. We will begin each with a short prayer and end each with a stirring rendition of 'God Bless America' sung by a different member of our talented armed forces. You know, the same ones we see all the time during the seventh innings of baseball games. Let us begin.

"God, we ask you to allow the United States of America to once again achieve the high place it deserves in our wondrous world. We have so many blessings in our great country, and we beseech Thee to allow us to have more. We want You to let Your abundance reign down on our treasury....erm....I mean, our treasured sheeple....erm....citizens. Thank you. Amen.

"This will not be a long chat, ladies and gentlemen, and children too. Kids, I hope you are watching with your parents. I know this is not as much fun as playing Kill the Asian Zombie, but some sneaky son of a bitch teacher may spring a surprise quiz on you, and you want to be prepared. I also welcome those who call themselves gay. That is to say, people who are happy. Queers can go bite each other. All the he/shes, and she/hes out there, you transsexuals should be playing Kill the Asian Zombie instead of watching Significations and Redemptions. Not only do you not have any religion, you are not really human. You're sort of caught between a rock and a soft place.

"It is vitally important for Americans to know what I stand for. I hate wishy-washy quasi-humanitarians. I also hate it when citizens express fear and doubt. That is what liberals do. If an IRS agent comes to their door, they hide under their beds. For all their talk about helping the poor, the average liberal has hundreds of thousands of dollars hidden under their mattresses. I read this in *Goldman's Magazine*, and I have no reason to doubt its authenticity.

"What can I do for America? Do not ask me that. I have a novel idea for you. A great American once said, 'It is not what I can do for you, it is what you can do for me.' That is what you need to do. And together we can do it to each other. I feel a revival preacher's energy and inspiration when I speak to you, my brethren....erm.... my citizens.

"I believe in policies.
I believe in opinions.
I believe in significance.
I believe in programs.
I believe in activities.

I believe in management.
I believe in advancement.
I believe in enhancement.
I don't believe in enchantment.
I believe in teamwork.
I believe in sovereignty.
I believe in success.
I believe in business.
I believe in oil.
I believe in policy programs.
I believe in justifications.
I believe in significations.
I believe in redemptions.
I believe in sub-committees.
I believe in plans.
I believe in progress.
I believe in growth.
I believe in the sub-committee to plan for progressive growth.
Alleluia!

"I pledge to you my commitment to this sub-committee, because I firmly believe that our past was the gateway to our present. We must pass through this wondrous gateway that is our present to get to our bright future.

"Thank you, ladies and gentlemen. Now to end our program, accompanied by the Norman Nabertwackle Choir, Private First Class Enrique Gunderson III will sing 'God Bless America.'"

# 9

# Removing Skunk Odor From Republicans

## Skunk odor removal

After a day spent at the Republican National Convention, delegates often return with a scent that can make them outcasts. Want to remove skunk odor and bring them back into the home? Here is a recipe for a homemade solution that works to remove the odor. Use it within one hour of mixing because it loses potency quickly. Discard any unused solution after application.

**GOP Tea Party senator raising his tail during a filibuster**

□ **Skunk odor can be transferred from your Republican to your furniture.**
□ **Most Republican shampoos will only temporarily mask the odor. The recipe below actually removes the odor.**
□ **When Republicans are in a group, they don't recognize that they stink. It takes an outsider to give them proper perspective.**

# Homemade Republican odor-removal solution

¼ cup baking soda
1 teaspoon dish soap
1 quart 3% hydrogen peroxide
Double the recipe for large Republican governors
such as Crisp Christley

# Applying the Republican odor-removal solution

Put the Republican odor-removal solution directly
on your Republican. Do not add water or get your
Republican wet before applying the solution. Work this
solution into the coat and over the skin. Carefully avoid
the eyes. Apply to the head with a cloth. Leave the
solution on for 5-20 minutes.  Keeping his/her eyes
closed should be easy, since they are rarely open.
Rinse thoroughly with water.
Wash with a Republican shampoo of your choice,
working the shampoo well into the skin and hair to lift
any grease, bacteria, vermin, blood stains, or oils.
Rinse thoroughly.
Apply Republican conditioner.

# Additional tips for removing Republican odor

For Republicans with severe, direct hits, reapply the
peroxide odor-removal solution.  Tea aggravates the
odor.  Rabid Tea Party members may not be able
to be rehabilitated.  You may have to bury them in the
backyard, at least twelve feet deep, covered with lye and
peat moss.  For Republicans normally trimmed at the
groomers, have them trimmed to remove lingering
scent trapped in the hair.

Supplement with products that replenish the skin oils stripped by hydrogen peroxide: *Nordic Un-Naturals Omega-9 Republican*, and *Be Square for Republicans*. Reapply topical flea and tick products in 24 to 48 hours, because they are stripped from the coat along with the Republican scent.

To help your Republican's skin and coat return to normal after all the scrubbing, feed Omega 3 fatty acids. You must watch your Republican closely for the next 24 hours. They may want to return to normal society too soon. Remember, they are unaware that they stink.

"Who sent me this! Rhoda, get me the State Department! No, get me the Defense Department! No, make that the CIA, the NSA, and the FBI! This looks like Senator Sandcastle's work!"

# 10

"**R**hoda, it is time to address healthcare. I want you to call a press conference tomorrow morning. The first thing we will do is remove the word 'care' from all the programs. There is healthcare, Medicare, Obamacare...Who the *hell* cares? We need new designations. Now, the Surgeon General title is cool. It sounds like the king of doctors, a guy who can really wield a scalpel. Let me see...I suggest, instead of Medicare, we call it the Pharmaceutical Distribution Agency. We need to remove oversight from the U.S. government, privatize it back where it belongs, and give control to our friends, the drug and insurance companies. We can no longer afford to treat every poor person who gets cancer or who has a fucking hangnail. We need to return the for-profit model into every facet of American life if we are to survive in our brave, post-humanitarian plutocracy.

"What I am going to propose to Congress is a drug distribution system that is based on the ability to pay. The very wealthy can get, and deserve, any top-flight drugs that are available, even those made in small quantities. It is their money that funded all the research in the first place. The middle class, what is left of it, can use the generic versions of those same drugs, if they are available. The poor can use over-the-counter drugs or, if they cannot afford those, they will be given experimental drugs that have not yet been approved by the FDA. (By the way, I am going to disband the FDA, but I will get to that another time.)

"If experimental drugs are given to the poor, it is a win-win for the rest of us. Drugs can be brought to market quicker because the testing does not need such rigorous protocols. We can bypass years of animal research. Think of all the monkeys and white rats that will get a new lease on life. Grand breakthroughs can happen much quicker than before. Speed will save lives. It takes courage to sacrifice the few for the many. The poor who will die will definitely not bother us, and their kin will probably feel all noble that they helped with the scientific research, especially after the drug companies slip them a few thousand dollars for funeral expenses.

"I am going to recommend the following protocol changes to take effect immediately. I do not need congressional approval. I will use Executive Privilege.

1 – I intend to stop all 'wellness' examinations. That is a ridiculous notion. You do not need an exam if you are well. You need one if you are sick. Insurance companies are losing billions of dollars. Yes, it amounts to billions of dollars with this preventative care nonsense. Doctors, hospitals, and drug companies are supposed to treat you if you are sick, not prevent you from becoming sick. That is why our medical costs are so high. All this time and energy is being wasted on well people. It is absurd. Another way of looking at it is that sick people *pay* to get well. They are the ones who the system is designed to serve. We cannot fill our hospitals with well people.

2 – The poor and middle classes will have an extra 30-day waiting period to see the doctor of *our* choice. This extra time will clarify many conditions and cut down useless triage. Those sheeple who

did not know their diseases were advanced will probably die, and the system saves all that treatment money.

3 – Malpractice insurance will no longer be necessary for our doctors.  It is a contradiction in terms to allow it in the first place.  We refer to a doctor's profession as a 'practice.'  That implies trial and error.  How can you get good at something if you do not practice?

4 – Hospital stays will be reduced so more sheeple can be processed.  Acute care, with dozens of specialists, costs more than lengthy hospital stays where only one or two doctors and nurses are in attendance.  More sheeple brought through emergency rooms means higher profits for the hospital and staff, which equals a more robust economy.  It is so simple.

5 – The word 'Medicaid' will be stricken from all documents.  It is a travesty.  When you put a band-aid on something, it is a quick fix, something that is not going to last.  Plus, AIDS is a disease that is almost always fatal. The word-association with *aid* is most unfortunate. The idea of treating people for free is an even worse disease.  Do you have any idea how many sleek F-35s we can build with that money?

6 – I am going to propose graduated insurance rates.  I got this idea from Senator Sandcastle, who always rants about a graduated income tax and raising the cap on Social Security.  All you have to do is look at the medical charts.  Which group gets sick the most often?  Which group is the most unhealthy, has the worst nutrition (whether or not they can afford the right foods is not the question here), has the lowest life span and the highest infant mortality rates? It is the poor, that is who.  Does it not make the most sense if the poor carry the highest insurance burden?  I propose a

reverse graduation of insurance rates. The healthy rich should not have to pay for all those destitute, illegal-alien sickos."

# 11

"Senator Sandcastle, I gathered the data. Here's the report you requested."

"Excellent, Jennifer. Let's see what you discovered, or should I say *uncovered*, since we're dealing with slimy creatures that live in the dirt."

"Item one. Vice President Percy Floy is currently planning on getting marijuana approved in Iowa. He has a shadow company registered in his wife's name, and they are planning on huge profits from converting what was once prime corn-growing territory into pot fields and strip malls.

"Item two. My inside source tells me that the first family's relationship is rather shaky. There's a lot of bickering between husband and wife, between the children, and between the children and the White House staff. The whole family has a group session every week with a psychiatrist who is disguised as some kind of journalist.

"Item three. My White House source also told me that the president sneaks out at night to a rendezvous with Foxxy Hart. In other words, he's cheating on Rhoda Dendron, who is the person he has been seeing instead of his wife.

"Item four. Hades plans on doing away entirely with Social Security and Medicare. He's going to replace them with privatized programs. However, companies that employ fewer than one hundred people will not be eligible. In essence, if you do not work for big corporate America, you will not be able to get medical attention or retire."

"Great work, Jennifer! I hope you are protecting your source. If he or she is found out, Hades and his bunch might get ugly. Floy is a lightweight. It will be easy to submarine his efforts in Iowa. He has the governor and legislature in his pocket, or so he thinks. What he's not counting on is the religious far-right. We will spread the word about the evils of marijuana smoking to every priest, rabbi, and minister in Iowa. Get the staff busy on that as our first action item. They will put so much pressure on their state legislators that not even Percy Floy will be able to pass the measure. That will mean all his land and silo investments will tank. He has a reputation for becoming unglued when thwarted. He will make bad mistakes we can then exploit.

"As for Hades' extra-curricular activity, I suppose we can say what Jan McDrewer said in her debate with Floy, that if he can't be true to his family, he can't be true to the nation. But I just can't bring myself to nail him. In any case, that strategy didn't do McDrewer any good in the debate. What a person does after hours, even slime-balls like Floy and Hades, should not be judged by you or me, unless it compromises national security. Mmmmm, Jen, see if you can get a handle on *that* idea. If Ms. Hart gets exclusive information that is 'leaked' by the president, we can definitely do something about that.

"We also can't publicize the fact that the first family is seeing a shrink. There will be as many people who support that as there are against it. As a matter of fact, he will gain points with moderates, something we really don't want.

"As for Social Security and Medicare, I'll bet he will delegate that to Floy. Hades isn't stupid. If the GOP rebel under pressure from their constituents, and the plan backfires, he can blame it all on the vice president while keeping *his* hands and record spotless. However, we're not going to let that happen. Guess who I'm having lunch with next week."

"Who?"

"Nora Hades, the Dragon Lady herself. She called me personally yesterday and said her conscience was bothering her, and she wanted to clear the air about something."

"Be careful Bernice, this smells like a trap."

"I know you're trepidatious, Jen, but don't worry about me. I'm very good at looking perplexed, vulnerable, even helpless and frightened by the powerful person who is trying to intimidate me. Little do they know I carry a .44 magnum in my purse. I'll let her lead me to where *I* want to take *her*. Then I'll squash her like a bug."

"Do you really carry a .44 magnum in your purse?"

"What do you think? Oh, I've got a good joke. Where can you find a Republican politician who's not currently taking bribes?"

"Where?"

"The cemetery."

# 12

"**R**hoda, it is past time to address violence in the United States of America. I would like you put out another press release. I read in the *Daily Kos* that Germany and the United Kingdom each have about 80,000,000 citizens. In the past four years – now I say again, this statistic is not annual but a four-year - fewer than four sheeple have been shot and killed by police in the United Kingdom and Germany combined.

"What do the sheeple *do* over there, sit in cafes watching each other eat knockwurst and crumpets? America has a pulse, those who are left alive, that is. I could never live in a place so completely devoid of action. You cannot demand martial law if the sheeple are not unruly. I do not know how their heads of state can get anything done. How do they ban occupy movements, large protests, or picketing outside corporate headquarters if no one is armed or creating a disturbance?

"I am proud of the Pasco, Washington State Police Department. Here is a small U.S. city with only 67,000 residents. In the last six months, they have killed more sheeple than police have in the United Kingdom in the last four years. Wow, that *is* something to be proud of. On February 10th they killed an unarmed man who was throwing rocks. They have now instituted a ban on throwing snowballs, and citizens throwing snowballs while wearing a hoodie can be shot on sight. I agree with this new action. You can hide rocks inside snowballs. Did those stupid anti-gun liberals ever think of that?

"I am going to contact the Army Disbursement Corps of the Defense Department. I want to issue surplus flamethrowers to the Pasco police for them to use against vicious snowball attacks. If we have any Abrams tanks we can spare, send them along as well. Make sure they are snowball-proof. I am especially concerned that some twelve-year-old girl could jump up on the tank and stuff snow in the muzzle of the cannon. This may cause it to explode when fired. Make sure the tank-tops are electrified with high voltage.

"The arms we produce for the military, if not used, can find new homes with our domestic police forces. This is creative diversification by our military/industrial/government complex. I do not want to see unemployment rise. I hate to say it, Rhoda, but domestic tranquility equals economic depression. How can we afford to stop producing weapons? Plus, there are too many sheeple in the world, and most of them are poor.

"If the Pasco police can kill four, imagine the totals when Detroit, Chicago, St. Louis, New York, Newark, and other major cities are factored in. I will bet our police kill more citizens than the rest of Europe combined. I have decided not to address gun violence after all. Things seem to be in balance. If it is not broke, do not fix it. More sheeple die in gun violence in America in one year than all the soldiers killed in Afghanistan and Iraq since the beginning of those wars.

"We *are* number one! Take that, you stupid Russians!

"Rhoda, get your assistant to send the following letter to the Pasco Police Chief:

"Dear Chief, thank you for your staff's dedication to preserving law and order at all costs. I sincerely hope that the rocks thrown by that.....minority person.....did not seriously injure your officers. I hope there is no bruising from the grazed shoulder and, most important, I hope the trigger fingers on all your right hands are still in good health. I am sending some neat equipment for you to test on the snowball throwers."

All the best,
Nick Hades

President, United States of America

# 13

"**Y**ou never look at me any more since you started having breakfast every morning with Rhoda, you unfaithful son of a bitch. Breakfast, I'll bet it's breakfast, and I'm sure you just love her buns with a little butter."

"And the fact that you jump into bed with your Secret Service minder while our children are in the White House is a mere oversight, you *actual* bitch."

"You can't prove that, Mister Impotent President.  At least the Secret Service dudes know where their private parts are located. You're getting so fat from your goddamn Sunday ham, you can't even find yours."

"I am getting fat?  Nora, you stopped looking like Twiggy one week after we were married.  Cannot prove it?  Is that right?  What do you think I had installed on the new light fixture in our bedroom ceiling?  Watching you is better than the watching the porn channel, you slut."

"You're disgusting.  I may have put on a few, but to a normal man, that would just make me more interesting.  Have you noticed your dragon tattoo lately?  As your belly expands, your tattoo is getting all stretched out and sickly pale. That dragon looks about as formidable as a dead garter snake.   You're going to have to go back to Indonesia for a touchup. What are you going to do, put a tattoo artist in your cabinet? At the rate you're expanding, he will have to travel with you on Air Force One."

"Do not you worry, bitch, I will have my pick of traveling companions on Air Force One, under my Oval Office desk, or on the billiard table, and none of them will look like your horse-face."

"Am I supposed to feel slighted and left out? I feel relieved. See, Dr. Gung, he tries to make me feel guilty by excluding me from his daily activities."

"I understand how you feel, Nora. How does her last comment make you feel, Mr. President?"

"*Feel,* that is a good word. She is incapable of feeling, unless someone probes her with an iron crowbar. She just cannot stand it that I have more power than she has. All our married life she has always needed to be the center of attention. Everywhere we go. If she cannot talk louder than everyone else, she will grab her trombone and blow it. If that does not work, she will take off her clothes and turn tricks in some barely hidden corner the guests can watch. She hates it when my press secretary sits close to me."

"Nora, do you feel threatened by Rhoda Dendron?"

"No, not at all. I'm pissed off that a frumpy, pineapple-shaped little pimple like that can hold our mighty president's interest. Do you know why? Because it proves he has no taste. What does that then say about his choosing me for his mate? Actually, I know why, it was my parent's money. That's what put him through law school. He planned on getting rid of me afterward, but we had

Petunia, who believe me, was a huge mistake. He was afraid my father would kill him, so here we are."

"I feel we've done some good work here today, and we're making real progress. I would like to see the two of you next week, in addition to our family meeting, at the same time, if your schedules allow."

"Next Tuesday is not good, because we are hosting a dinner for Reverend Norman Nabertwackle to celebrate his network of Christian homes for unwed mothers. Nora and I are really looking forward to that meeting. The reverend married us in Indiana and has remained a lifelong friend. Our children just love him. Is that not right, dear?"

# 14

"**R**hoda, my survey is ready for the American sheeple. Many democracies have used the national referendum to give sheeple a voice in how their respective heads of state should proceed on important issues. However, as you know, we have a representative form of government. The individual congressmen and senators speak directly for the sheeple, who do not have to show up in Washington to speak to me personally. At least I hope not. They all vote fairly as their constituents would want them to. I love that word *fairly,* as in *almost* or *nearly* or *not exactly.* It is so close to the word fairy, as in la la. In Tea Party districts, you will not find many esoteric philosophy majors whose voices need to be heard. I think our system works great as rebuilt, after redistributing the voting districts. Troublemakers need to be ignored and left out of the process. Now it is truly fair by my definition.

"When you want to accomplish something, first do the opposite to let the sheeple think you are pulling for them and care about their concerns. Then you can discard those concerns with the usual double-speak and do exactly what you want.

"My ruse is to go directly to the American sheeple and ask them their opinions on ten important subjects. Since Karl Krotch is Secretary of the Interior, and owns most of this country's media, I will ask his help in collecting and tabulating the data. This will do two things.  One, it will give the sheeple the impression that I care what they think.  Two, it will tell me what the pulse of the nation really is so I can take appropriate corrective action to bring the sheeple back into my fold.  The questions themselves are a way to guide the sheeple into the right opinion 'pen.'

"Here are the questions.  They will be put online and broadcast into all cellphones, portable devices, newspapers, and television news shows nationwide.

1 – Is your family better off now than in 1935, when a Democrat was president?

2 – Would you like to be protected from foreign invasion, but do you also welcome foreign cold, hard cash?  Do you see a contradiction here?

3 – Do you want the federal government to tell you which drug to use for your bipolar disorder?

4 – Do you feel safer if your family is protected by automatic weapons that are kept in your front closet?  (Child locks are optional here.  We do not want to over-regulate.)

5 – Are you sick and tired of some bureaucrat telling you how much gas mileage your car should be getting?  Would you not feel safer in something bigger than a Hummer?

6 – Do you resent getting notices about your electric power consumption?  Do you feel free to turn the thermostat up to 88 degrees, or does some PBS news person send you on a guilt trip?  Do you know or care how solar radiant heating works if it is more expensive than good old heating oil?

7 – Do you trust Chinese products as much as American, especially since most American products are now made in China?  Does it make any real difference to you, especially if the Chinese products are much cheaper?

8 – Do you want Chinese, Arabic, and Swiss taught in our public schools, or should we stick to English?

9 – Do you want the Federal Government to keep your Social Security money, where it gets absolutely no interest, or would you like The Bank of American Commerce to make you much richer with their skillful speculation?

10 – Since our student debt is now over 1.16 trillion dollars, do you support sending graduates into the Army for four years to pay off their debts, or do you want them to remain freeloaders living at home with their parents?

# 15

"**W**elcome, welcome. Sit anywhere you like. You all know my chief of staff, Rhoda Dendron. The other members of my cabinet are nationally famous and need no introduction. Once again I have asked our most senior and respected member, Senator Jim McCann of North Dakota, to lead this session. He is chairman of the Armed Services Committee.

"Fellow Rat Packers, I have invited these four fine people to join us today because their input is, quite frankly, as important to me as yours. For too many years, government has existed in a vacuum without counsel from the greatest minds in American business. We get pontifications from inexperienced pontificators who pontificate in liberal think-tanks. They happened to be lucky winners in some unimportant New England state, and we have to hear them on the Senate floor filibustering about how oversized the Pentagon budget is, but we hear nothing from the very people who built this country.

"So, from right to left let me introduce Mary Ellen Nonsense of Lockness Marin; Junco Inman, of Standard Electric; Dribble J. Lesser of Hallitosis; and Crug Picknose of Brownwater. Before we begin, I do not insist that you turn off your portable devices and phones while at our meeting. However, if you do get a call or text message, please plug your device into this combination projector-amplifier for us all to hear and see. Transparency and full disclosure are high on my priority list. We owe that much to the American sheeple....erm....citizens.

"In a private meeting last week, Senator McCann expressed concern that our F-35 program was lagging behind, and vastly over budget. Now you know I am all for using American money for guns, but I would like to get the best bang for the buck. All four of your companies make parts for the F-35, and Lockness Marin is doing most of the manufacturing. Jim, would you like to start us off?"

"Concern is a mild word, Mr. President. I'm furious! I have direct combat experience flying jet fighters, and I know a turkey when I see one. Compare the F-35 with the F-22. There's no contest here. A pilot in an F-22 will smoke two F-35s in air-to-air combat. The F-22 is the best in the world. Look at the stats:
F-22, maximum speed, Mach 2.25, 1,500 mph
F-35, maximum speed, Mach 1.6, 1,200 mph
F-22, combat range, 1,840 miles
F-35, combat range, 1,135 miles
If the damned F-35 can't fly as fast or as far as the F-22, what the hell good is it?"

"Jim, I hear you have some reservations, but I think we should look at the positive...."

"Excuse me for interrupting, Mr. President, but 'reservations' doesn't describe how I feel. Let's put me down for outright opposition. I hate to raise my voice, because I feel when you lose your temper you lose your power, but we know why this fucking plane is being built, don't we, Ms. Mary Ellen Nonsense! Lockness Marin stopped production of the F-22 after intense lobbying efforts. Our last president and secretary of defense were sold a bill of goods. What a crock. We all know the real reason, Ms. Nonsense. By United States law, the F-22 can only be built for domestic use. We can't export this great plane even to our closest allies. The F-35, on the other hand, is going to be built and shipped to Canada, England, Australia, Italy, Norway, The Netherlands, and many other countries. That's why the F-22 was cancelled. Do the fucking math! We plan on building 3,200 planes at a cost of 140 million dollars per plane. *That* is the reason why the F-22 was cancelled. And to add insult to injury, they plan on replacing two other great planes, the A-10 Warthog and the F-18 Super Hornet with this turkey."

"Jim, you are beginning to be a pain in the ass. There are other issues and considerations here. What is the good of having a great plane if we are the only ones that can use it? By sharing our technology with our friends, we become much more formidable. In unity there is strength. Plus look at the economic benefits of the F-35, which is why I called this meeting in the first place. You are right about the cost overruns. I want to find a way to reduce that 140 million dollar price tag, and I am going to open the floor to our distinguished CEOs for their input and ideas. Yes, Ms. Nonsense."

"Thank you, Mr. President. I propose the following changes to the F-35 contract. As you know, our friends at Standard Electric make many of the components for the plane. However, they have outside contractors that supply them with many of the parts. They make a tidy profit because they pay less for the printed circuits, onboard computers, and other equipment, but still receive full compensation from the government.

"What I would like to do is offshore manufacturing of the F-35 to China. We can oversee production just like we do with our toasters, televisions, and cellphones. The sensitive equipment that Standard Electric provides can be manufactured in India or Mexico. We then import each module into our main assembly center in Fort Worth. I project the savings to be at least 85 percent. However, I don't suggest we reduce the plane's cost the entire 85 percent. We can pass 10 percent back to the taxpayers, 35 percent to our stockholders and CEOs, and 40 percent to our friends in Washington. What do you think, Junco?"

"Sounds like a win-win to me, Mary Ellen. Our board of directors will welcome your proposal. The only glitch we have so far with our offshored missile-fire-control software is that it's written in Chinese. We do give each pilot a Chinese-English dictionary for a quick translation during engagements. It shouldn't be a problem."

"That is the kind of spirit I want from the leaders in this room! I do not want to hear reasons why we cannot do something. I want creative solutions that will actually work. Where and when do we start?"

# 16

"**P**ercy Floy, vice president of the United States. How does that sound to you, Percy? I told you if you were patient, it would come to pass."

"Pretty damned good, Mr. President, pretty damned good. Listen to this. The company I put in my wife's name just purchased twenty small grain-storage facilities in Iowa. We also have 25,000 acres of prime tillable farmland at the ready. The governor and state legislature owe me favors, and now that I'm the vice president, I can call them in. They are going to make marijuana legal in Iowa. Corn is so yesterday. Washington and Oregon think they are very cool, making pot-smoking legal. But they don't have the resources that we have in Iowa. Our climate is much more conducive to growth. The crop takes much less storage space, and the yield-per-dollar-per-acre is 150 times greater than corn. The land that we don't use can be converted to strip malls and tract housing. There's money to be made there as well. I don't give a shit about drought conditions. We can pipe in water from Saskatchewan, right alongside Keystone.

"I've got to ask you a question, Mr. President. Were you serious about Jan McDrewer? I wondered about that debate...."

"Serious? Shit no. Not a chance. She was just a stooge placed on the stage to make you look good. Your staff did a great job exposing her for screwing her professor. That is the kind of leadership I need you to bring to the Senate. You will be standing at the presiding officer's desk. You're the guy who will run the place. I know you do not have a vote unless there is a tie. That is not going to happen, because we have a fifteen-seat majority, but you still wield tremendous influence. Are you happy with the role of heavy? I need someone to break knees on occasion, metaphorically speaking, of course."

"Bernice Sandcastle is my first victim...I mean target...I mean *person* to whom I will devote my attention, sir, if you know what I mean."

"Excellent choice! She is always stirring the pot. PBS loves her, and so far I have not been able to cut their funding. The guy I put in charge of the FCC has some ideas. We have to use the socialist's own policies against them. I will give you an example. Franklin Delano Roosevelt's name is cursed by every red-blooded American who believes in laissez-faire. His WPA has become the holy program for socialists like Sandcastle as an excuse to take money away from those who rightfully own this country.

"Did you hear her latest diatribe? She was effusing about the Germans. It seems they have offered free university tuition to Americans and other foreigners living in Germany. Since she opened her big mouth and publicized that fact, the Germans will be expecting the same thing in return. Not a chance. Instead, I intend to cancel all import tariffs on RatsGroggen Ale. Quite frankly, the shit tastes terrible, not nearly as good as our worst light beer, but it is a gesture that will win favor. Now they cannot say we did not reciprocate.

"This is what I would like to do, and I want you to use your Senate power to set things in motion. As you know, our infrastructure is kind of limp at best. Our bridges are rusting, and compared to Europe and Asia, our rail systems are antique. We are going to propose a program we will call the New WPA. However, before we do, we will alert our friends at Hallitosis, Standard Electric, National Steel Center, and another dozen major construction companies about our plans, so they can be ready to exploit the situation. We will offer a win-win to the American sheeple.

"Here is how it is going to go down. We put out a huge publicity campaign about how this administration is going to do something to fix America. At the same time, we will put sheeple to work who have not had jobs in years. Where will the money come from? From the American sheeple, where else? Socialists want big government to take care of their every need, and that is exactly what we are going to do."

"But how do we come out on top, Mr. President?"

"This is how. We offer jobs at minimum wage, with no medical benefits. We will just make sure that they pay more than the average welfare check. By the way, we are going to launch an attack on that system as well. If there is no 'safety net' for the freeloaders, they will be forced to work for the New WPA. So we publicize the fact that any work is better than drawing a small welfare check. Our friends at National Steel get cheap labor paid for by the taxpayers who are actually doing the work. In a sense, they are being taxed twice. The money goes to the top of each company, and a good deal of it is kicked back to us. We rebuild the country in the process. A neat by-product is that we can use some of this labor for vacation home renovation, clubhouse refurbishment, or other lawmakers' needs. What do you think, Percy?"

"You're a genius, sir!"

# 17

"**Y**ou know, Percy, you do not have to call me Mr. President unless we are in public. From now on it is Nick and Percy."

"Thank you, Mr. President, I mean, Nick. Guess who I heard from this morning? Do you remember the twins I told you about? One of them told me they will be in Washington tomorrow and wanted to know if we could get together. Is this something you might be interested in, a frolicsome foursome?"

"Most definitely! Let me see those photos. Whoa, they are both stunners. Do you have any preference? Which one do you like better? They are not identical twins, so there are some differences."

"Makes no never mind to me, Nick. As far as I'm concerned, women like them are like wild horses. You ride 'em hard and put 'em away wet. I'll set it up for Friday night."

"Great idea! Hey, we can entertain them right here. Nora and the kids are going to the Fashion Night gala, and by five thirty most of the staff will be gone. I will just make a phone call saying that we do not want to be disturbed, and we will have the place to ourselves. By the way, what are their names?"

"I don't know their names. I asked them, and the only thing I could get is Number One and Number Two. Imagine that. They lived in my guest house for two months, and I don't know their names. They said remaining anonymous makes the sex kinkier. It was so good, I didn't want to rock the boat, if you know what I mean."

The time is eight on Friday night.

"How did you get in here, I mean, past security?" President Hades asks Twin Number One.

"As you can see, Mr. President, we're dressed in Daughters of the American Revolution costumes. We told the guards that we were late for a photo op with Percy. They smiled and let us through. It seems nobody will question women carrying American flags and wearing poke bonnets with ruffles. Wait till you see what we have on under the costumes."

The twins rip off their garments. "What do you think of that, boys?"

The evening progresses quickly. President Hades is aware that they have only until 12:30 before everyone comes home from the gala. The champagne flows freely. In two hours they are lit and ready for fun.

"I know," Percy says in a loud, playful voice, "let's go out on the roof. I put a huge air mattress up there, and we can see the stars while we get it on. No one will see us up there."

Madeleine Soufflé observes the foursome walk up to the roof. She discreetly follows them. She has a professional-quality Zeiss digital camera with a fast 1.2 lens.

"We like playing with your bellies, reminds me of home, sliding down a mountain of snow, whee, right into the belly button. Now we conduct navel maneuvers. Now we go further down and....oops....missed the big guy, it must be hiding in there somewhere. Where is your guided missile, Mr. President? Is it hiding in your silo? I know how to launch it.

"There it is. Oh, it's definitely not an ICBM, more like an MRG-3 Little John, or maybe a Sidewinder. It *is* a little crooked. Okay, Twin Number Two, are you ready to launch rockets?"

"I am ready, Twin Number One. We press this button and...hooray! We have ignition."

Saturday morning, just before breakfast, Rhoda Dendron brings in the morning papers. But today she is livid and her face is bright red. There on the front page of the *Washington Post* are a dozen photographs of the president, vice president, and the twins doing their thing on the White House roof. At that moment Percy Floy comes tearing into the room.

"It is not what you think, Rhoda, I will take care of this. Please give us some privacy.

"What do we do now, Nick? We're screwed. We don't even know their names."

"The first thing, Percy, is to remain calm. We do not know who is behind this, but as with everything else, I suspect Bernice Sandcastle. Wait, I have an idea. Do unto others as they did unto us."

President Hades picks up his special phone. "Hello, give me the CIA Director's office. This is the president, and this is an emergency."

"Hello, sir. Yes, I saw the papers, Mr. President."

"Ralph, this is what I want you to do. You have the best Photoshop people in the world. I want you to create some similar photos using Senator Sandcastle and her staff. I know it is a bit over the line, but hear me out. I am going to admit that the photos are fake, and I will not say where we got them. I am going to use them to prove a point. I need them by the end of the day today, at the latest.

"Here is the plan, Percy. On Monday I go out on the Senate floor just after we post the CIA-made photos on the Internet. I admit to everyone that the photos are fakes, just like the ones that some anonymous traitor sent to the *Washington Post*. This will make people doubt their authenticity.

"Give me those photos of the twins. I am going to email them to NSA Utah. That place is my favorite building. They have a huge database, and they have something on everyone. Let us see who these girls are. It should not take more than ten minutes. They work very fast. We need to find out right away, and we need to get something on them so there will be no more trouble. How much money will it take to keep them quiet?"

"They're as poor as WalWart employees. It shouldn't take much, Nick."

"Okay Percy, we have something back from NSA Utah. Their names are Ludmila Kasyanenko and Natalia Bulgakov. Oh shit, they are not twins, and they are Russians.  Fuck!  I did not lose my National Security cellphone; one of them must have stolen it.  Nobody can find them.  I have got the CIA, the FBI, NSA and an Interpol APB out, but they have disappeared.

"Damn!  Percy, they lived in your house for two months.  Did you not suspect that they are not Americans?"

"They looked like Americans, you know, white skin and blue eyes.  They never spoke Russian.  Well, they did say 'da' a few times, but I thought they were talking about their father."

Sunday passes like an eternity for Hades and Floy.  On Monday morning, the floor of the Senate is quiet and tense, and the gallery is packed.  Extra Capitol Police are on hand in case they're needed.  President Hades walks up to the podium.

"It is a sad day when perverts deliberately falsify photographs and send them to what was once a respected newspaper.  I say *once*, because they have proven that they are irresponsible.  *The Washington Post* has refused to reveal the source of those photos, but I am going to make it a treasonous offence if they do not.  When I find those responsible, they will serve very long jail times.  Are you listening to me, Senator Bernice Sandcastle?  You are my prime suspect.

"As all of you can see, photos were posted on the Internet this morning that showed Senator Sandcastle and her staff in compromising positions, performing unnatural acts.  These photos were deliberately faked to prove a point.  This should prove, beyond any doubt, that someone from her office did the same thing to demean me and my administration."

"Just a minute, Mr. President, you just admitted to deliberately demeaning me and my staff. I don't care what kind of point you're trying to make. That is against the law and *you* will be prosecuted."

"Sorry Sweetie, my executive powers allow me to defend the Constitution, and that includes the right to free speech. It is called the Tat for Tit statute, and you are the one who violated it."

"And how, exactly, could I fake the way that dragon tattoo looks on your belly? I dare you to take your clothes off and expose yourself to the American people. They will see what's real and what has been doctored."

# 18

"**W**hat did you want to see me about, Nora?"

"Well, Bernice, things have changed since I made that appointment for us to meet. You may find this hard to believe, but they've changed for the better."

"I'm not stupid, Nora. You know full well that the President and I are locked in mortal combat over actual and doctored photos. This is a fight he can't win."

"You're right, Bernice, but it's also a fight he can't lose. This one will be a draw. The American people will not believe in either set of photographs because of the *possibility* that they're doctored. So, in a sense, he will have negated your efforts. By the way, you have a very good mole in our den. I wonder who that person is?"

"Since we're off the main boulevard and traveling down side streets, Nora, I might also mention that you have an interesting relationship with your Secret Service detail."

"Really? Of course I will not confirm or deny that, but I also hear that you don't have any sexual practices at all, that your public display as an androgynous neuter is your private display as well. That's a clever way to stay off FLOX News."

"You're probing, Nora. My suggestion is to turn off the side street back onto the main boulevard. Why did you want to see me? You called this meeting before the photo-war started. By the way, Nick really should do something about that tattoo. It's ludicrous. How can you stand his behavior? And palling around with Percy Floy, for God's sake. He's a sub-moron. You know it's just a matter of time before they destroy themselves and unravel for the whole country to see. Certain personality types can't rise above their own excesses. All the people have to do is be aware of them. That's what my newfound calling is. I am now a holy socialist warrior, and my job is to pull their pants down in public. Of course, they've done that to themselves already. Now what the hell did you want to see me about?"

"To get right to the point, Nick covered all his bases as he rose to the top. He's once removed from all kinds of trouble. If this photo charade doesn't go his way, it won't touch him. Good old Percy will be thrown to the sharks, and Nick will be morally outraged by his behavior. He has alienated Jim McCann by calling him a pain in the ass in front of the entire cabinet. He's trying for damage control, but Senator McCann won't take his calls and has resigned from the cabinet. This has got Nick pacing the floor, trying to decide on the best course of retribution. When he's worried, he always talks to me about it just before bed. That's how I know when he's in some kind of deep shit. In other words, he's once removed from everyone except me."

"Nora, why are you telling me this? What does all this have to do with *me*?"

"It's very simple, Bernice. We have never had a female president, let alone a president *and* vice president. Although mainstream, corporate America considers you part of the lunatic leftwing fringe, you are gaining support among moderate Democrats. You have a good chance of beating the saccharine, middle-of-the-roaders in the primaries. You're going to need a running mate who can get things done. This is where I come in. With me on the ticket, switching from the Rethuglicans to the Democrats, I will bring a whole bunch of votes you could never otherwise get. In the vice-presidential debates, I will chew up and spit out whoever they put up there against me. Plus my family has real estate holdings in all 50 states, and enough money to counter the Krotch brothers."

"You can't be serious! Sandcastle/Hades? You can't be serious!"

"No, not Sandcastle/Hades. It will be Sandcastle/Hilton. I intend to reclaim my family name after I throw Nick out. It's past time to change the chief executive's gender. No need to give me your answer now. Think about it. By the way, did you ever meet our family chef, Madeleine Soufflé?"

"No, why?"

"She's very talented. I would call her a Renaissance woman. She's as much at home with a Zeiss digital camera as she is with a food processor. I like Madeleine and I intend to keep her very close.

"Keep in touch. We'll talk soon."

# 19

"**P**etunia, did you do your homework?"

"Yes, Mother. It's all done except for my political science class, and I'm working on that now."

"Oh yes, I didn't see your book. I thought you were texting your friends. We never had political science in high school. Do you like the teacher?"

"Frau Hymnler? I think she's an ultra-religious fascist. Don't forget, you didn't live in Washington, D.C. and your father wasn't the president. Do you have any idea how much pressure I'm under? Everyone looks at me before I speak, expecting me to say something brilliant. Even fucking Hymnler leans on the edge of her chair, waiting for some profound statement."

"She said it again, Mom. No video games or cable TV for you tonight, Pizza-Face."

"And none for you either, Alfonso. *Pizza-Face* is now in the same category as the word she used. Petunia, has that class got you all tensed up?"

"Not really, I can handle it. We were given a list of political terms and asked to define them. Wanna see what I've got?"

"Sure, go ahead."

Autocracy = A lunatic Honda

Accord = A larger Honda

Affirmative Action = Watching your yes-men perform

Bilateral = A woman who goes both ways

Bipartisan = A man who goes both ways

Chairman = Two steps below Sofaman

Color Guard = People who will not fade with repeated washings

Credentials = False teeth that move

Defeat = De feat are in de shoes

Defense = De fense is around de yard

Demagogue = Where ten Jews go to pray

Democracy = Where ten mentally ill people are locked up

Gerrymander = A man who changes color depending on his surroundings

Impeach = A former president's least favorite ice cream flavor

Laissez-Faire = Light-skinned people who don't want to work

Mandate = What congresswomen are really after

Paradox = Two physicians

Pigeonholing = I'd rather not say

Private Person = A person who does his dirty work where no one can see him

Quorum = Your side has more money to buy votes

Lobbyist = A pervert who hangs out in hotel waiting rooms

Muckraker = Nerd capitol interns who have to clean the bathrooms

Ombudsman = The White House gardener

Plutocracy = A demented planet

Post Nationalism = A country obsessed with breakfast cereal

Pragmatism = A vision problem where things don't line up

Proletariat = A Triple-Crown horse that finished last

Republic = Meeting the same people over and over again

Republican = People who came back to the pub to lick garbage cans

Rotunda = A very fat senator

Superpower = An outstanding laundry detergent

Supreme Court = Oxymorons

Theocracy = Some lunatic named Theodore

Titular Nation = What immature American men long for

Trickle Down Economics = When people don't quite make it to the bathroom

Veto = He starred in *The Godfather*

# 20

"**O**h Rhoda, that is no way to be. You know they were just a diversion. You are my main squeeze."

"What about Nora?"

"She too, on occasion. After all, she is sort of my wife. But let us not talk about my family. I really love our breakfast meetings, especially since I put in this huge folding couch. You and I are the only people, besides the anonymous sheeple in Procurement, who know that it folds into a king-sized bed. Here, have some French toast, maple-cured sausages, and fresh-ground coffee. Mmm, delicious.

"We have six papers to go through this morning. You read three, and I will read three. As is our custom, we will each bring up what we feel is interesting. We get so many good ideas this way. I must say that this morning has a lot better-looking *Washington Post* front page than last week's. Sheesh, that was a major nuisance, but it is finished now. Sandcastle is smart enough to know that she will alienate sheeple if she takes it any further. She wants my job. I can smell it.

"You would not believe how many interns and staffers have gone out of their way to visit me in the last few days. I am more popular than ever. Now, do not go getting all jealous. Most women respond to money, power, or fame. When a man has all three, plus a neat dragon tattoo, I guess he is basically irresistible.

"We always love to go through the business sections. I love it more than sports, the arts, national news, almost anything. I have learned one very important fact that I see repeated over and over. Creating an artificial need for products through speculation is the only way to make real money.

"The lowest form of labor are the sheeple who actually do the work: plumbers, truck drivers, doctors, farmers. The next lowest form are the sheeple who teach others how to do those things. One step above the teachers are those who invest in the labors of others. But the highest form of all are those who use other sheeple's investment money to create wealth for themselves. These are my people, the speculators.

"The most basic premise in advertising is to create a need for a product where none exists. Sheeple need food. This is very basic, but how can we make money? The hardest part is already done. We do not have to create a need, so we do not have to advertise. Without food, sheeple will starve. Here, have some more French toast.

"Rhoda, have you ever stopped to think why the *Mona Lisa* is so valuable? I will tell you why: because there is only one in the entire world. There is no other painting like it. If daVinci had painted 200 of them, exactly alike, they would be worth but a fraction of the multi-millions that the original is now worth. When there is a surplus of something, like food for instance, and it is very cheap to buy, people all over the world can fill their bellies without impoverishing their families. Food is then hardly a valuable commodity.

"This is a situation that we do not want. Our Republican corporate investors, our Wall Street banking friends, and the Krotch brothers all profit when food is expensive. We accomplish this by synthetically driving up the prices of soy, wheat, poultry, fruit, and other produce. Naturally, the money does not go back to the farmer, or even the supermarkets that sell the food. Do not forget, they are the lowest form of labor in our hierarchy.

"No, the money goes directly to those who are adept at speculation. We have insider information from our executive privilege that tells us what food products are going to be manipulated. As prices rise, the food becomes more desirable and precious. Since sheeple in the Third World still need this food, they will pay exorbitant prices to stay alive. Some will die, but that is not a speculator's problem. That is a UNESCO problem, or for some other humanitarian organization to handle. As far as I am concerned, speculators cannot be blamed for following profits. That cause is as noble as healing the sick, even more so.

"*Speculation*! The very word stirs my soul with excitement. Before I was president, speculation used to involve tremendous risk. There was a danger of serious loss. The cliché used to be, without risk there are no rewards. One of the things of which I am most proud is that I have taken the risk out of food speculation. Now prices can rise unchallenged to reach their absolute pinnacle. The American sheeple have been totally fooled. They think food prices are rising very slowly. What they are not aware of is that the five-pound bag of flour is now four pounds. The 26-ounce jar of tomato sauce is now 24 ounces, and the price is up ten cents. We are creating jobs. All that new, deceptive packaging must be designed and manufactured.

"Once again, mighty American Wall Street speculators lead the world. Have another sausage?"

# 21

# Controlling Republican Cockroaches

## GOP cockroaches (*Periplaneta Americana*) are in control of our military/industrial complex

Republican cockroaches can absorb more radiation than any other living creature and still survive. That is why they aren't afraid of war, even nuclear war. They stand to inherit the Earth. You can count on them to reduce healthcare budgets....I mean, do you seriously think that a Republican cockroach cares about your health? They will always try to divert our healthcare money into defense spending.

**GOP cockroaches discussing their budget**

We cannot live with these vermin. We cannot

placate them with offerings of moldy cheese. The roaches won't go away unless they are voted out of office. When you see bumper stickers that say, "We support GOP Roaches," shun these people. Do not enter any home with a GOP Roach campaign sign. You may immediately become a carrier and take one of the filthy little fuckers home in your pants cuff or your handbag.

Unfortunately, they have a newly developed immunity to the old insecticides. Getting rid of GOP roaches is not impossible, but can be somewhat difficult. We gladly share our tips with you.

GOP cockroach after losing election

# Roaches can go more than a month without food but no more than a week without water.

Put away all foods and make sure your kitchen is spotless. Do not leave dirty dishes soaking in the sink. GOP roaches thrive in a filthy ecosystem, and they are especially attracted to grease, oil, and gold. Plug up all leaks in your home, especially in your basement. Stop delivery of the *Wall Street Journal* and *Money Magazine*. The roaches will leave your home in search of a GOP household with these publications.

# Use GOP cockroach greed to cause mass suicide.

We normally would never suggest giving a drug addict drugs, an alcoholic liquor, or a gambler a ticket to the race track, but since this is our nation's biggest scourge, we must be creative in our approach. GOP roaches love your sugar. They love to steal your sweets and add them to their own larder.

# Mix boric acid with the sugar and place the mixture near their congressional offices.

The roaches will be attracted to your sugar. Little do they know that you have mixed in boric acid. They will eat the mixture and, well, the only good roach is a dead roach.

☐ **Republicides may be used with caution. We suggest Cyfluthrin.**

- ☐ GOP cockroach traps are effective. Make sure the trap looks like a Wall Street bank.
- ☐ Chairmanships can be used as bait. Bait and switch them out of office.
- ☐ Roaches hate soap and water. It suffocates them by clogging their pores. They then die from ethics violations.
- ☐ GOP roaches can also be found in the Supreme Court and in our governors' mansions. Apply Republicides liberally.
- ☐ In Florida, the GOP residents try to pass the roaches off as "Palmetto bugs." Do not be deceived. Roaches are called by many other names, such as Majority Leader or Speaker of the House. But a roach is a roach.

# For help dealing with GOP roaches, please send for our free pamphlet

Contact Bernice Sandcastle – United States Senator, Vermont

"I am going to kill her!"

# 22

"**A**lfonso, why are you up at two a.m.?"

"I don't need much sleep. I always get up in the middle of the night to play video games. I use my headphones so I don't wake up Pizza-Face in the next room. Why are you up?"

"I could not sleep either. I was wondering what to do about Iran, Israel, Syria, Lebanon, Iraq, and Libya."

"Why don't you just bomb them all? You're the Commander in Chief. I think it would be neat."

"Alfonso, you cannot just bomb every nation you have a disagreement with."

"You wouldn't have to. After bombing the first couple, the rest wouldn't disagree with us any more."

"I wish it were that simple. What kind of video games do you have?"

"You wanna play one? Why don't you choose from these three."

"Mmm, I will read the descriptions by Jinny Gudmundsen, Executive Editor of *Video Games*, and then decide."

**_Dead Space 3_**: Not only do you kill thousands of alien creatures using an assortment of weapons, but they can also explode into red chunks, rip in half, catch on fire, and be dismembered and decapitated. The heroes, too, can die a dramatic death in slow motion, including being cut in half or decapitated. You'll also see execution-style murders and suicide. As with the two earlier installments in this series, _Dead Space 3_ is an extremely violent, bloody, gory, and scary action game.

**_God of War: Ascension_**: This game is a nearly nonstop series of intensely graphic, highly visceral combat scenes involving a wide range of fantastical beasts. Few games feature blood-soaked battles with more severed body parts or spilled innards. It's gory enough to make even media desensitized grown-up gamers occasionally whistle in disbelief. Players use sharp-edged melee weapons -- chain blades, swords, and spears -- as well as blunt weapons like mauls and hammers to not just kill, but also eviscerate their enemies. The game also carries some mature sexual themes and the game's protagonist is so vengeance obsessed that he kills just about every creature he comes in contact with.

**_Call of Duty Black Ops II_**: This gritty, extremely violent military first-person shooter involves constant killing using realistic weapons, with blood and gore pouring across the screen during more intense scenes. Cinematic sequences can be even more dramatic and graphic, with soldiers and civilians alike dying in horrible ways, including graphic melee kills, people burning to death, civilians killed in crossfire, torture, and a shipping container filled with rotting corpses. In one scene, the player steps into the shoes of a villain and goes on a murderous rampage against soldiers, the screen turning red with blood rage as he takes damage. This M-rated game also has frequent profanity, some sexual themes and drug use.

"So, what do you think, Dad? I suggest Call of Duty, Black Ops II. If you think Sniper was good, wait until you see this. It's very realistic because they use American weapons and drugs. Plus, it might give you some ideas on how to handle the towelheads."

"Good idea. Black Ops II it is. How do you work this thing?"

"It's a Zombie console and controller. You put your fingers here, so you can be in the best position to go left and right, or up and down. That red button is your kill trigger. The computer feeds us alternate views at random. The player who kills the most people wins. The neat thing about this game is that civilians killed in crossfire or by torture count in the total. Some stupid games subtract points for civilian deaths. Are you ready? Here we go."

# 23

"**J**ennifer, you would not believe the conversation I had with Nora Hades. I need time to digest what she said before I can even discuss it. Talk about bizarre!

"Let's prepare now for those special elections in Indiana and Kansas. As you know, Indiana's Democratic senator is retiring due to health issues, and in Kansas they didn't achieve a plurality so they must hold another gubernatorial election. The Repukelicans are favored in both races. Indiana is Hades' home turf so it's going to be tough to put in another Democrat. We don't have much money, but we do have the ability to put out information. The entire staff brainstormed your original idea. I think it's a brilliant turn-about. I only hope the people are capable of understanding sarcasm. It's so outrageous, they can't possibly take it at face value. At least let's hope not.

"Okay, this is what we've got."

Ten reasons why you should vote Republican in the next election:

1 – You don't like minorities. People of color in charge of the government are a threat to the American way of life. They will favor their own and turn out the very people who built this country.

2 – You don't want anyone telling you that you must have affordable medical insurance. You get what you pay for, and if you want the best, you must pay for the best.

3 – Corporations are run by people, people who should be counted. There are hundreds of thousands of professionals who know more about politics than minority people who get in line for handouts.

4 – You don't want the government handling your retirement money. They cause trillions of dollars of waste, and the nation is badly in debt as a result. The Bank of American Commerce should invest the money in derivatives to eliminate the red tape that is costing the taxpayers millions. Why should the government guarantee your retirement security? The government simply can't be responsible for your every need.

5 – You want to redistribute funding away from student loans, healthcare, and sustainable energy into military procurement of F-35s, new missile submarines, and more army generals. The world is a dangerous place, and we need to be number one at all costs. What good is it to have educated students if we're overrun by Arab savages?

6 – Electric cars are totally unnecessary. Who wants an engine that sounds like four chipmunks spitting? Oil made this country great, and we should open up exploration along every American coast, and in every national park. Sure, there are some environmental risks, but energy independence, the ability to drive your V8 Hummer whenever you want, as fast as you want, is much more important. Americans should not have to pay more than $2.25 for a gallon of gas, no matter what is going on in the rest of the world.

7 – You are sick and tired of old liberals on the U.S. Supreme Court.  With Republicans firmly in place in all branches of government, conservative men and women will replace the retiring progressives.  You can repeal Roe v Wade, make prayer legal in all our public schools, and bring back compulsory military service.

8 – Not only are you against the immigration laws proposed by Democrats, you want to deport those illegals who are already in this country.  No citizenship?  Get the hell out.

9 – You believe the food stamp program has outlived its usefulness.  It isn't the government's responsibility to care for every poor person in the country.  That is the job of our church charities.  The money saved can be used for oil exploration.

10 – You want tax relief.  Estate taxes, capital gains taxes, and graduated income taxes have stifled initiative and turned America into a country soon to approach third-world status.

"Mmm, you know, Jen, on second thought, it's not a good idea to put this out.  It would clinch a Repukelican victory.  Let's save it for Vermont or Massachusetts whenever they hold their next elections.  They know the meaning of irony there."

# 24

"**R**alph, you did a great job with the photographs. I told you we would admit to their being doctored. I have another job for the CIA, and this one is legal. As you know, we just passed Homeland Security Rider 213B. We tailed it in with the National Parks Maintenance Budget and put it to a vote late Friday afternoon, so we had no trouble getting it through in a light session. In case you do not remember the fine points, it reads, 'The Executive Branch of the United States Government may take preventative action if a citizen is suspected of crimes against the citizens.'

"Posse comitatus, Habeas corpus, Malum prohibitum, Delerious delectae, who cares about that Latin bullshit. This is not Rome, this is America, and we do not need that legal mumbo-jumbo. It is my job to protect the citizens, and now I have the opportunity.

"So Ralphie, old boy, what this means is that if I suspect that a person may be up to criminal activity, I can head them off by any means necessary."

"Mr. President, do you need a court order?"

"Absolutely not, no court order needed, and no congressional approval. Sometimes we have to move quickly and cannot afford to get bogged down in partisan bickering.

"To get right to the point, Senator Sandcastle has an informant in the White House. I have hundreds of staff members and cannot fire them all. This is a direct threat to national security. What I want you to do is infiltrate our staff and find out who it is. Since Sandcastle is our prime suspect, I want you to bug her car, her office, and the office of her chief of staff, what the hell is her name, oh yes, Jennifer something or another. This should be an easy assignment for your best professionals. Sandcastle does not believe in tight security. At any given time there are dozens of tree-huggers parading in and out of her Washington office, and also in Vermont. It would be a good idea to bug her offices there."

"Yes sir, we'll get right on it."

Meanwhile......................

"Jennifer, Nora Hades knows that Madeleine Soufflé took the photos of Laurel and Hardy up on the roof. Dragon Lady's not telling him about it because she wants to bring him down. This will work in our favor, but we have to be careful. I wonder what the famous duo will be up to next?"

"Oh my God, we've started a war."

"Oh, you mean with Dickens and Fenster, or is it Abbot and Costello? Not to worry, Jen. Actually, those men are great comedians, but Hades and Floy aren't a comedy team, they're a two-headed amoeba. Did you hear that McDougle's is offering a Percy Floy Hamburger? It has no meat, only two sticky buns with butter."

"I like that one. Do you know why President Hades' pants have a faux zipper? It's because there's nothing in there.

102

"Bernice, my friend Tom is an Army intelligence vet. I asked him if he could get some bugs, not cockroaches, but listening devices for Madeleine to plant in Hades' office. He said yes, and she said she could place several. No one has a better opportunity than Madeleine does, especially with Nora Hades looking the other way. The receiver is built in to my custom cellphone, and it automatically records what's being said. It works within a five-mile radius. What do you think?"

"By all means, it should be a laugh a minute."

The results are in................................

"So, Ralphie boy, what did you find out?"

"Mr. President, we were successful in planting five listening devices in the locations you requested. I will play back the high points."

"Excellent! Let us hear them in action."

*"Jen, I've got three letters from returning vets who don't have access to healthcare. It seems the Republican Sequester has cut back visiting hours at their local clinic, and they have to wait months for treatment. This is shameful and dangerous. Make a phone call to the hospital and insist that they be seen right away."*

*"So you see, children, this is where your lawmakers work. This is my office, where important decisions are made that will affect you and eventually your children. This is your heritage, and it's very important that you and your parents safeguard it, because it's precious."*

*"Let's introduce a bill to ensure that net neutrality is a permanent fix. We don't want a few mega-corporations to have control over the most important medium in the world. It must remain free, not sold to the highest bidders with the highest volumes."*

*"Today is February 15th, Susan B. Anthony's birthday. She was born in 1820. She has always been one of my favorites, Jen. If there is anyone in history I would have loved to talk to, it would be her."*

"Whoa, wait a minute, Ralph. These are the high points? Is this all you could get?"

"This is all so far, Mr. President."

"Well, keep at it."

And...........................................

"Bernice we've got some sound in the can! It's kind of hard to understand; you have to listen very carefully. Madeleine put a bug in Hades' Sunday ham. Her idea is that he would swallow it and we could hear what he said no matter where he went. That worked up to a point. When he and Floy are talking in the Oval Office, it sounds like his ham is at war with the stale beer in his internal sewer. I'm afraid too much is lost."

*"Number one and number two were seen (gurgling) with Vladimir Putin (gurgling) handing him a small package that probably contained your (gurgling)."*

*"Shit! That sucks. Now we have to change all the (gurgling) so the (gurgling) is not compromised."*

*"So far we have gotten (gurgling) on Senator (gurgling). So we must be patient and give the (gurgling) time to (gurgle)."*

"Jen, here's my gut reaction, ha fucking ha. I suggest that Madeleine place another bug in a different spot. I don't want to think about where this one will go next."

# 25

"**P**etunia, Alfonso, listen to me, and listen good. I know you don't like official functions, but you're going to this dinner whether you like it or not. The president of the Southeast African Republic has two children, and they're about the same age as the two of you. He made a special request that you be present because his wife and children will be accompanying him. You're to be on your best behavior all evening long. This country is very important right now because they've given us a drone base to attack terrorists on the entire African continent. Do I make myself clear?"

"Can I bring my video game, phone, iPod, and............"

"Nothing, Alfonso. Neither of you will bring anything except for the presents you're to give to his children."

"Mom, if I don't know what the presents are, how am I suppose to pretend the gift is from me?"

"Petunia, I have no time for your endless questions. Your father will brief you on the details. Now I must leave to help him make final arrangements. Oh, and one more thing. Alfonso, I want you to hear this as well. There will be no outrageous dress. Before either of you is admitted into the dining hall, you'll be inspected by me. Is that clear?"

"How will *they* be dressed? What if his kids show up in some kind of native garb, you know, towels on their heads, sandals and no socks, or bones in their noses?"

"Alfonso, that's quite enough. Don't push your luck. If you don't play well at this dinner, you won't be playing with anything for the rest of the year, I promise you."

Later...................................

"I had no idea they would be so dark, and I just knew they would be dressed weird."

"Alfonso, you're a moron. They're from Africa, what did you expect them to look like, Austrian yodelers? They're Muslims. You're supposed to show some international awareness, if you can ever get your stupid head away from those video games. You're becoming truly and completely warped."

"Not everyone from Africa looks like them, Pizza-Face. The Dutch from South Africa look different, so do the people from Israel. Jews don't wear towels on their heads. They wear those miniature beanies. You think you're so smart. I may be warped, but I don't carry a rug and towels around with me everywhere I go."

"Sheesh, not so loud, we don't want them to hear your stupidity. If you don't shut up, you will be playing with yourself for the rest of the year."

"Oh yeah? I'll speak as loud as I want. Dad is right. Towelheads can't be trusted, and neither can their kids. What the fuck did they bring *us*? They come to dinner all the way from Borneoland, and don't even bring so much as a bar of chocolate. Dad should do what he said the other night when we were playing Black Ops II. We should bomb them back to the Stone Age. They all look like orangutans anyway. What do they need cities for? We should stop pretending that they're important to us."

"Alfonso."

"Yes, Mom?"

"Will you please come outside with me for a minute? Right now!"

"In a while, Mom. Right now I would like to stay right here and enjoy the freak show. Where's my fucking hamburger?"

# 26
## Itch McCringell
## Senate Majority Leader

**Place and date of birth:**
August 8, 1942, in Stillwell, Alabama.

**What did your parents do?**
My father was a door-to-door vacuum cleaner salesman, and my mother used the vacuum.

**Where did you go to college?  What was your major, and your most valued accomplishment?**
My undergraduate work was at Stillwell College, and my graduate work was at the Colorado School of Mimes.  I majored in Greek accounting and minored in birds.  My most valued accomplishment was becoming editor of the *Farcical Obstructionist*.  It was our political newspaper.

**First job after graduation?**
When I graduated School of Mimes, my first job was as a Naysayer on the Stillwell City Council.

**How did you meet your mate?**
Oh, that's a happy memory.  I was in the drug store looking for hemorrhoid cream, and she came out from behind the counter and handed me a box of suppositories instead.

**What are your favorite books?**
*Valley of the Dolls*, and *Mitch Mitchell and His Flying Machine*.

**What is your favorite music?**
I love German opera sung in American.

**If you could be anywhere in the world, and with any person in history, where would it be and who would you like to be with?**
That is a very good and thoughtful question. I would like to be on a very tiny island somewhere in the South Pacific, with Cleopatra, Mata Hari, Joan of Arc, Marilyn Monroe, and Lizzy Borden.

**What is your favorite food?**
I like Chinese and Italian food with American pork-barrel gravy.

**What is your favorite movie?**
*Bambi,* and *The Texas Chainsaw Massacre.* It's hard to choose between those two.

**What is your favorite TV show?**
*Dancing With the Degenerates.*

**When you have two hours for yourself, what do you like to do?**
I like to bicker and argue with my family. Whatever they say or do, I say and do the opposite. It's great training for my work in Congress.

**If you could change one thing about yourself, what would it be?**
I have one very annoying habit. I keep doubting myself when there is absolutely no need to.

**What is your ultimate ambition?**
To be President of the United States.

**How do you want to be remembered?**
As the best President the United States ever had.

# 27
## Jboo Boehnhead
## Speaker of the House

**Place and date of birth:**
February 7, 1949, in Middleburgh, Ohio.

**What did your parents do?**
My parents owned a poodle grooming and nail clipping salon.

**Where did you go to college?  What was your major, and your most valued accomplishment?**
My alma mater, both for my bachelor's and master's degrees was The Middleburgh College of Social Research.  I majored in Stem Cell Trading.  I guess the thing I'm most proud of is that I lost my composure only three times.  Considering the dozens of classes I took, that was quite an accomplishment.

**First job after graduation?**
Gee.  My first job was very difficult, and I have a hard time talking about it without cry.... well, never mind.  I was a facial-tissue tester.

**How did you meet your mate?**
We were at a Democratic fundraiser in Cleveland.  We had each brought eggs to throw at the speaker, but we bumped together, the eggs broke and trickled down our legs.  That's when I knew I would marry her, make a lot of omelets, and be a lifelong Republican.

**What are your favorite books?**
*Controlling Your Emotions*  by Doctor Rodney Steiger.

**What is your favorite music?**
I love all the Wayne Newton live-in-Las Vegas concerts.  I also like his brother Fig's music.

**If you could be anywhere in the world, and with any person in history, where would it be and who would you be with?**
I would like to be marooned in a lifeboat with plenty of food and water, and with three people: the guy who invented the three-piece business suit, the guy who invented paper money, and the guy who invented the cloth handkerchief.

**What is your favorite food?**
I like a balanced diet, one that goes with my alcohol, tobacco, sugar, and caffeine addictions.

**What is your favorite movie?**
My three favorites, in no particular order, are *The Cornelius Vanderbilt Story*, *The Muppet Movie*, and *Bedtime for Bonzo*.

**What is your favorite TV show?**
*Beverly's Hillbillies.*

**When you have two hours for yourself, what do you like to do?**
I like to replay the best speeches I've made through my speaker collection. I have a 10-inch, 12-inch, and even a special 15-inch coaxial speaker. My best speeches I play through all of them at once for a 360-degree surround sound. It's awesome. If you don't praise yourself, who will you praise?

**If you could change one thing about yourself, what would it be?**
I'd try to tone down my macho image. I know I frighten people, and I must learn to be more sensitive. I've made enemies with my fierce stare and intimidating facial hair.

**What is your ultimate ambition?**
To be President of the United States.

**How do you want to be remembered?**
As the man who rewrote the past.

# 28
## Ludwig Peckeroff
## Secretary of State

**Place and date of birth:**
June 9, 1934 in Dufusberry, Iowa.

**What did your parents do?**
My mother made corncob pipes, and my father was a standup comedian who specialized in cornpone humor.

**Where did you go to college?  What was your major, and your most valued accomplishment?**
Dufusberry College of Arts, Sciences, and Corn.  I majored in business agrarianism and minored in business agrarianism.  I feel very proud that I really knew my corn by the time I was finished.

**First job after graduation?**
It was a typical job.  I worked in a gas station.  My job was filling the gallon jugs.  We had a still in the back room and made corn likker.

**How did you meet your mate?**
We sort of ran into each other in a cornfield.  We were both hunting grouse.  I had a 20 gauge shotgun, but she was using a powerful 12 gauge.  I knew right then and there that she was the woman for me, and that the word "bang" would be our favorite.

**What are your favorite books?**
*Global Warming Is Just a Hoax* by Doctor Slight Lee Quacked and *Bat Shit Man Goes to Congress*, I forget the author.

**What is your favorite music?**
Oklahoma is the place for prairie music, oil field music, and tornado music.  I love all of those.

**If you could be anywhere in the world, and with any person in history, where would it be and who would you be with?**

I have always wondered what life was like in ancient Rome. Were those baths really coed? Did they really have oil-rubbing orgies in the Pantheon? Were their soldiers so tough that they slept on the bare ground? Did the senators have shotguns? I would love to visit the past.

**What is your favorite food?**

Corn dogs.

**What is your favorite movie?**

You had better mean movies. There's a bunch of them. *Oklahoma, God's Little Acre, Ridin' Shotgun, The Boll Weevils of Osage County, The Pride and the Fury*, and *Snow White*.

**What is your favorite TV show?**

I like the soap opera, *The Young and the Useless,* and the science series *Cosmotology.*

**When you have two hours for yourself, what do you like to do?**

I like to load my own shotgun shells. For grouse I use #6, for rabbits I use #4 shot, for deer I use double-ought buckshot, and for Whooping Crane I load heavy slugs. They can be fierce.

**If you could change one thing about yourself, what would it be?**

I am trying to be more down-to-Earth. I get the feeling I'm constantly being criticized for my abstract thought, and my ability to enter and juxtapose different philosophical dimensions. I don't want to alienate people by being an elitist.

**What is your ultimate ambition?**

To be President of the United States.

**How do you want to be remembered?**

As the man who successfully predicted the next Stone Age.

# 29
## Sarah Lapin
## Chairman, American Association for the Advancement of Science

**Place and date of birth:**
April 23, 1964, Darjeeling, Idaho.

**What did your parents do?**
My Mama had an earthworm farm, you know, those big suckers for fishin', and my Pa taught hunter safety courses at Darjeeling High School.

**Where did you go to college?  What was your major, and your most valued accomplishment?**
Darjeeling Military Academy. I majored in reading tea leaves, and minored in beauty pageant preparation.  I was a point guard on our basketball team and was one rough bitch.  I earned the nickname Sarah Lunatic for my erratic and unpredictable play.

**First job after graduation?**
My first job after graduation, and actually it was my first job until after I was married, was running for Vice President of the United States.

**How did you meet your mate?**
We were both fishin' off a pier in Bristol Bay, and the dumb-ass snagged my line.  It took so dogone long to untangle that I guess we sort of fell in love.

**What are your favorite books?**

*Uncertainty: The Life and Science of Werner Heisenberg*, by David Cassidy, and *Quantum Reality: Beyond the New Physics*, by Nick Herbert.

**What is your favorite music?**
I love heavy metal, light metal, especially aluminum and titanium. But shucks, gold will always have a special place in my heart.

**If you could be anywhere in the world, and with any person in history, where would it be and who would you be with?**
Golly, I never thought about that. I would like to have been standing next to Galileo when he first saw the rings of Saturn. I believe he was quoted as saying "Holy shit!"

**What is your favorite food?**
Baked Alaska king crabs with Tabasco sauce, mustard, a big pinch of jalapeño pepper, and a pot of party tea.

**What is your favorite movie?**
*Annie Get Your Gun.*

**What is your favorite TV show?**
*House of Cards.* It's so much like what I remember in my political career.

**When you have two hours for yourself, what do you like to do?**
My favorite pastime, bar none, is shooting wolves from my helicopter. I got my pilot's license, and I've become quite adept at tilting the chopper with my left hand while I shoot the wolves with my right. If you think that's easy, try shooting a .44 magnum revolver while you watch your rotor trim.

**If you could change one thing about yourself, what would it be?**

Not a thing.

**What is your ultimate ambition?**

To be President of the United States.

**How do you want to be remembered?**

I want to be loved for my mind as well as my body.

# 30
## Dwayne Lapoopierre
## Director, Bureau of Alcohol, Tobacco & Firearms

**Place and date of birth:**
June 17, 1948, Powderville, New York.

**What did your parents do?**
My father invented the electric rattrap, and my mother used the family .22 to kill all the rats that eluded my father's trap.

**Where did you go to college?  What was your major, and your most valued accomplishment?**
Powderville College of Ministry.  For five years I studied to be a minister in The Church of the Trampoline, but the peace and quiet nearly drove me crazy and I had to bust out.   So I guess my most valued accomplishment is that I didn't kill anyone while in school.

**First job after graduation?**
I have fond memories of my first job.  It was to arm and organize the Powderville day-care grandmothers.  Some of those five-year-olds can get very unruly.  I taught them how to triangulate their targets and to shoot instinctively.  A low aiming point was essential in their work.

**How did you meet your mate?**
She was a guest on my TV show, *SlimeKill*.  She told the nation how, as a woman living alone at home, she single-handedly killed seven teenagers who broke into her condo to steal her television.  I knew she was the woman for me.  She could share my home and guard my gun collection.

**What are your favorite books?**

*Gun Digest, Firearms Digest, Rifle Digest, Bullet Digest, Handloading Digest, Incapacitation Digest, Bleed-Out Digest*, and my favorite of all is the *Shit Hits the Fan Digest*.

**What is your favorite music?**
I love music with loud drums, pounding, slashing, crashing, thumping, and slamming.

**If you could be anywhere in the world, and with any person in history, where would it be and who would you be with?**
I would like to go back to 9th century China, talk with and observe that wonderful unknown genius who invented gunpowder. Did you know that he was an alchemist who was trying to find the secret of immortality, but he produced a grand explosion instead. The second person I would like to be with is Sarah Lapin, anytime and anyplace. I think she is so hot when she shoots her .44 magnum. This is off the record, so don't tell my wife.

**What is your favorite food?**
Marshmallows, flambé bananas, anything I can set on fire.

**What is your favorite movie?**
I invented a special device that is plugged into my entertainment system. It counts the firearm discharges in any movie or TV show. If there aren't at least forty gunshots during the first ten minutes of the film, it automatically shuts off and chooses another show.

**What is your favorite TV show?**
I already answered that question. Aren't you listening?

**When you have two hours for yourself, what do you like to do?**
I listen to the CDs I made at the rifle range. I have one of .556 assault rifles, another of .357 magnum revolvers, and one for semi-automatic .22 pistols. The .45 caliber submachine gun CD is especially exciting. I turn it up real loud and then put on my hearing protectors. It's the next best thing to being there.

**If you could change one thing about yourself, what would it be?**
Every so often I have a flyer. I'll shoot four rounds in a one-inch grouping at twenty-five yards, but the fifth will wander out another two inches. That expands the group of five to three inches. This is unacceptable for a man in my position.

**What is your ultimate ambition?**
To be President of the United States.

**How do you want to be remembered?**
I want to be remembered for bringing a sense of empowerment and accomplishment to the day-care grandmothers of Powderville.

# 31
## Adolph Krotch
## Chairman, U.S. Securities and
## Exchange Commission

**Place and date of birth:**
November 23, 1940, Capital, Kansas.

**What did your parents do?**
My father owned the town. It was given to him by my grandfather, so he really didn't have to do anything. I guess my mother was there at the right place at the right time, and she tagged along.

**Where did you go to college? What was your major, and your most valued accomplishment?**
Three years at Das Capital University, but then transferred to the Colorado School of Money for my senior year. Most people don't know it, but my degree was in social anthropology. I was going to join the Peace Corps. My most valued accomplishment is that I discovered the work of John D. Rockefeller, Jr. just in time, and changed my mind about the Peace Corps.

**First job after graduation?**
I engineered a leveraged buyout of seven family-owned businesses in Capital. How I did this was really quite ingenious. I bought the buildings where they had their shops, and then raised the rent so high that they couldn't afford to make payments. They then sold them to me for twenty cents on the dollar. That was the start of my financial empire, and I've never looked back.

**How did you meet your mate?**
It was a magical moment. We had each just bought some candy at the corner drugstore. We paid the same amount of money and were each

owed a dollar in change. When the clerk took out the first dollar we each grabbed an end. Neither of us would let go, and finally she wrenched it out of my hand. I knew she was the one. Any woman who could get a dollar away from me had to be a special person.

**What are your favorite books?**
*A Catalogue of Roman Coins, Ancient Paper Money of Vietnam, Beads and Talisman Wampum of the Plains Indians, Counterfeiting Through the Ages, Never Give Nuthin' to Nobody.*

**What is your favorite music?**
I like any music with grand symphonies. Those 110-piece orchestras remind me of my corporations.

**If you could be anywhere in the world, and with any person in history, where would it be and who would you be with?**
I'd like to go back to Mesopotamia in 3,000 BC. That's where money was first used. At the very moment that an ancient person used some shells or silver nugget to pay for something, I would have liked to grab it out of his hands and return back here to the present. That first money would be worth a fortune at Christie's or Sotheby's.

**What is your favorite food?**
I have 417 favorite dishes. My kitchen staff has a compete list. I guess it depends on my mood.

**What is your favorite movie?**
*A Christmas Carol.* Scrooge is so beautiful, in the beginning, that is. I also like *The Cornelius Vanderbilt Story.*

**What is your favorite TV show?**
*Wall Street Week.*

**When you have two hours for yourself, what do you like to do?**
There is absolutely nothing quite as soothing as listening to coins dropping through an automatic sorter. They all sound different, you

know. A penny falls with a thud. A nickel has a slight ting. A silver dime or quarter has a beautiful, almost enchanting ping. It lulls me into a peaceful sleep every time.

**If you could change one thing about yourself, what would it be?**
I would try to control my generosity and compassion for the common woman. I'm such a sucker if some twenty-five-year-old takes off her clothes and tells me her hard luck story.

**What is your ultimate ambition?**
To be President of the United States. And my brother could be the Vice President.

**How do you want to be remembered?**
As the man who made being filthy rich squeaky clean.

# 32

## Percy Floy
## Vice President of the United States

**Place and date of birth:**
July 29, 1959 in Place, Pennsylvania, which was the second state to join the Union. We later moved to Iowa.

**What did your parents do?**
My father opened the second pizzeria in Place. My mother was the second waitress he hired. They got along, so he married her.

**Where did you go to college? What was your major, and your most valued accomplishment?**
My first two years were spent at Place University, and for my final two years I attended the Pittsburgh Academy, which is the second oldest college in Pennsylvania. I majored in Political Science and minored in overcoming inferiority complexes. I was a good athlete. I got seventeen second-place finishes. My sport was boxing.

**First job after graduation?**
I interned for the law firm Alsoran, Notquite, and Secondario. I lost my first two cases.

**How did you meet your mate?**
After the person she was engaged to dumped her, she glommed on to me. I was her second choice, but since nobody else seemed interested, we made a go of it.

**What are your favorite books?**

*Nice Guys Finish Last; It's Not the Victory, But the Attempt; Not Everyone Can Be King.*

**What is your favorite music?**

I love elevator music.

**If you could be anywhere in the world, and with any person in history, where would it be and who would you be with?**

I would like to go back in time and be a first-place finisher in something. Even if I was the best murderer in town. I can't take it any more. I'm always standing behind someone.

**What is your favorite food?**

I'm not allowed to have any favorite foods, so I eat macaroni and cheese.

**What is your favorite movie?**

*Invasion from Mars.* I would help the aliens destroy Earth.

**What is your favorite TV show?**

*Ask Doctor Laura.* It's good to see people who are more fucked up than I am.

**When you have two hours for yourself, what do you like to do?**

I like to get real close to my bathroom mirror so that nobody can come between me and it. I enjoy staring at myself with everything in the room behind me.

**If you could change one thing about yourself, what would it be?**

I would learn how to sing and gyrate so I could be up on stage, with everyone looking at me, wishing they were me, jealous that they didn't have my money, looks, or talent. That's all I want.

**What is your ultimate ambition?**
Oh God! To be President of the United States!

**How do you want to be remembered?**
Who the fuck is going to remember me?

# 33

**D**r. Carla Gung doesn't normally go to the White House for counseling on a Sunday, but she was summoned there by Petunia because she was worried about her parents and felt there was an urgent need.

The Army-Navy basketball game was Saturday night, and the First Couple attended.  Normally the President attends the Army-Navy football game, but Hades thought he'd start a new tradition.  He gave instructions to the heads of both military academies on the new protocol.  Unfortunately, the results were not as expected.

"Mr. President, I've never seen you so angry.  What could Nora possibly have done to put you in such a rage?"

"Oh, nothing! Absolutely fucking nothing!  It is absolutely fucking, stinking, nothing."

"If it's nothing, why are you going off the rails, Mr. President?"

"Do you remember what I told you in an earlier meeting?  Do you remember that I said she had to be the center of attention no matter what was going on?  Do you remember that, Dr. Gung?"

"I do, Mr. President, but I suggest you calm down.  You can't be effective unless you remain calm."

"Doctor, the only time he's effective is when he's mute."

"Shut up, you bitch! I guess you did not see the news last night, or the photos on the front pages of every American newspaper! Last night we went to the Army-Navy basketball game. I started a tradition where the president and first lady would, as they have always done at the football games, switch sides during halftime. So for the first half we sat on the Navy side, and during intermission, we walked across the court to the Army side. The Navy color guard formed an arch halfway across the court, swords high, and the Army color guard formed an arch on the other half in a perfect, seamless line. So what does the bitch do? She drops her panties on the court right in the middle of the floor and casually steps over them. Naturally they were bright metallic red with shiny sequins. Every soldier and sailor in the stands cheered, and chanted 'Nora! Nora!' And what did she do, she grinned like a demented hooker on drugs, and waved to the crowd. That is all she did."

"You make such a big deal out of a simple accident. The elastic gave way. A gentleman would have just picked them up and discreetly put them in his pocket. You are a poor excuse for a husband. You have fooled the electorate, but you can't fool me. You're a little man with a little penis."

"And you are so big the only thing you can feel is a fire hydrant turned on to maximum."

"*Now* we're making good progress here, folks. It's important to talk about our feelings and what is bothering us. If we keep things bottled up, they will come back later to hurt us even worse. You must have been bickering rather loudly and upset the children. For their sake you should control your outbursts."

"Yeah right, they were probably having a knife fight in the next room, and we were interrupting their death and pornography video games. Nora has not taught them any discipline."

"Oh, so now it's my job to teach them discipline. And what exactly is your job?"

"I am president of the fucking United States, something you have not noticed. If you pull one more stunt like that, I am sending all three of you back to Indiana."

"Oh no you're not. You're stuck with us, *Mr. President.* I've go so much shit on you, not only would you be thrown out of office, you and your sidekick Percy would be thrown in jail."

"*Excellent* progress, folks. Looks like we've reached an understanding. I believe we can wrap this up until next week. Tonight why don't you all do something as a family? You can watch television together, or select a movie you all want to see."

"Dr. Gung, last week you suggested four different televisions to keep the peace. Is this called the scattershot approach? Or perhaps the sound you are making is the same one that a duck makes."

"Nick, don't take your foul temper out on her, she's just trying to help us. See you next week, Carla."

# 34

"**H**ere's the deal. If you don't want any more trouble from me, you'll give me a top-level position in the government."

"That is blackmail."

"No it isn't. It's paying a debt. I've stood there and smiled like an idiot every time you said the same thing over and over again to a different group of adoring poeple, night after night, in every state in the union. I've heard that speech so many times that it gives me nightmares, hot flashes, and cold sweats at the same time. You even campaigned in Indonesia! They don't even speak English, for God's sake. Doesn't that tell you something about your priorities? And you say *I* crave attention."

"So you want to make a deal. What do you want, a seat on the Supreme Court?"

"You know that job is too small for me."

"What else, then? Attorney General, Ambassador to the United Nations, head of the FBI?"

"No, not enough scope and power in any of those positions. They're okay, I suppose, but I would quickly tire of the limited possibilities. Plus, if the people vote you out, then I'm out too. This is what I want. As you know, there are three branches of government: Legislative, Executive, and Judicial. What I want you to do is put this through Congress."

Nora hands Nick a large folder, which he reluctantly opens.

"You want me to form a fourth branch of the U.S. Government, called the Absolute Branch. You want me to nominate you to run it for life!"

"That's the deal, or I'll squeal. Read on, you can see what else I want."

"You want your own headquarters no smaller than the Pentagon, and a staff of 7,500."

"Yes, think of all the construction jobs and specialists of all kinds we can hire. To a point, the Absolute branch has an equal say with the other three. After you sign a bill, for example, it must come across my desk for approval. If you veto a bill, and I approve it, tough shit, it passes. If you approve a bill, and I veto it, it doesn't pass. Do you understand the rules? I can't think of a better way for us to learn to work together. Can you imagine what we can accomplish if we agree on important matters?"

"This is an excellent idea, Nora, but I hate to say it, you have been scooped. I have already let out bids for construction of a Fourth Branch of Government building and I am not calling it the Absolute branch. It is going to be called the Omnipotent branch, and I will be in charge. It is a lifetime appointment like our Supreme Court. Some of those judges are narcissistic fossils who have jobs for life, even though they are egotistical non-entities who put out fossilized rulings. What if I don't win the next election? Or even if I do, in four years I would have to vacate the office.

Now I will be Lifetime Chairman of the Omnipotent branch, with full medical, travel, security, and retirement benefits. I will be King without the official title. This is your one chance to be Queen, so don't blow it."

"Omnipotent! You have got to be kidding!"

# 35

"**M**r. President, it's three minutes to air time. We're on a seven-second delay to weed out the crazies before they get to you, so that shouldn't be a problem."

"Thank you, Rhoda. How do I look?"

"Fine. Tie is straight, hair isn't messed. What's left of it, that is. You're good to go, please stand by."

"Hello, America. Welcome again to the Oval Office. This is the second of our nationally televised Significations and Redemptions chats. As we did last time, we will begin with a short prayer. This prayer was written by the Reverend Oral Fixation, of the Church of the Trampoline, right here in Washington, DC. 'Oh Lord, allow us to follow Thy abundance no matter where it appears in Your wondrous world. Teach us to avoid the back alleys of poverty and despair. Shine Thy sunlight on Thy golden treasures, and anoint our humble cobblestones with gold so they will enrich the path of Your righteous believers in this, Thy blessed flock, Amen.'

"My fellow Americans....wait a minute, that is a stupid thing to say, and I apologize. You are not all fellows. Some of you are female, probably about half, I would imagine. So I should say my fellow and gal-pal Americans, we are going to do something different in this chat. At the bottom of your screen you will see a phone number. It is your direct line to this custom-designed black

141

and gold phone on my desk. In order to avoid the massive electronic log jam that would result if everyone called at once, we are going to show a specific town, in a specific state, and put the phone number only for that town. Please do not try to reverse the charges, you will be automatically disconnected.

"As your president, I am vitally concerned with what the citizens are thinking. As that great American once said, and I quote him yet again, 'It's not what I can do for you, it's what you can do for me. That's what you need to do, and we can do it to each other.'"

Rhoda Dendron hands the president a note that reads, "The delay is not working. We are 100% live on all calls. Do you want to continue?" The president nods an affirmative.

"We are ready to take the first call from Cedar Rapids, Iowa. Just call the number at the bottom of your screen. Only Cedar Rapids callers, please. I have been informed that there are no callers from Cedar Rapids, so in the interest of time we will not wait any longer, and will move on to Salem, Oregon. As you can see, there is a different number on your screen....still waiting. No calls from Salem? Okay, let us move on to Helena, Montana. Still nothing? Okay, let us try Orlando, Florida. We have one caller from Orlando. What is your name and what would you like to do for your country?"

"My name is Joe the Jackhammer, and I work in construction, when I can find a job. Since there are no construction jobs in Orlando using my talents, I've had to do sissy work answering phones and waiting tables. All my physical energy is being bottled up. My anger is growing like bad air in an overstretched balloon. If you don't start building roads soon, and raise the minimum wage, you cock-sucker, I'm going to explode and blow your fucking head off!"

"Joe, you have a wonderful can-do attitude about wanting the right work. Have you ever thought about joining the military? They can use unbalanced lunatics like you who want to kill. We will give you some food, an automatic rifle, show you a photo of some towelheads, point you in the right direction, and you can make an enormous contribution to your country. Someone will contact you after we hang up. Next caller will be from New York, but only the borough of Manhattan. The city has millions of people, so you had better dial fast to get through."

"Thank you, Mr. President, my name is Harvey Schwartz from the *New York Times* and I would like......"

"Not you again! This program is for ordinary citizens, not pinko journalists. Do not bother me. To hell with New York City! Let us move on to Huntsville, Alabama."

"Mr. President, my name is Betty Median. Is it true that you always vacation in Indonesia? Why don't you use Camp David like all our other presidents?"

"Betty, I love this great country. We have the most beautiful scenery and the most outgoing and generous people in the world. But we do not have Komodo Dragons. A man must go where his heart leads him. Do you not agree? Next caller is from Odessa, Texas."

"Mr. President, my name is Howard Howitzer. I just want you to know that I think you're the greatest. It's about time we had a president who didn't want to take away our guns.  We really appreciate your support."

"You are welcome, Howard.  Not only do I not want to take away your guns, I want every American to feel he or she has the right to carry any kind of weapon, any place they choose to carry it.  That is the only way we will remain a free people.  At least, the survivors will be free.

"We have time for one more call from, let me look at my prompter, yes, it is from Burlington, Vermont.  On second thought, I had better not take any calls from that state.  Why do you not join the Canadian Federation, you left-wing bunch of electric car junkies, and stop annoying my administration.

"As I said in our last chat, I firmly believe that our glorious past was the gateway to our present.  We must pass through this wondrous gateway that is our glorious present to get to our bright future.  I hope and pray that we will all go there together.

"Thank you, ladies and gentlemen.  Now to end our program, accompanied by the Norman Nabertwackle Choir, with Wally Wanker on the conga, Lieutenant Junior Grade Shawna McTavish will sing 'God Bless America.'"

# 36

"**N**ot you, too? I just spent an hour arguing with Nora about it. Foxxy is moving into the White House because I need her to be my outside media contact, and it is a lot better if she is close by. Rhoda, you are my inside person. Do not get all jealous. We must safeguard our positions, and she will help accomplish that. Of course, we will have closed door sessions from time to time, but it is strictly so I can use her to leak information to the press. Speaking of leaking, that reminds me of something I have to do later on today after I get Foxxy settled in. Call Jboo Boehnhead and Itch McCringle and have them in my office at three. Thanks, Rhoda.

"Nora, please do not barge in when I am dictating to Rhoda."

"Dickbrain."

"Somehow I just knew you were going to make a dick comment. You are so predicktable. Foxxy will be staying in the Lincoln Room, and that is all there is to it."

"How long will she be staying?"

"Not long. We just need to formulate a good media outreach program. She brought a few things with her."

"Two Allied Van Lines semis full of shit! You've got to be kidding me!"

"Do not get your discarded red knickers in a knot. It is probably all office equipment. She will have full use of the White House swimming pool, library, bowling alley, gym, basketball court, and movie theater. The only condition I made is that she does not write about those things. I do not want the American sheeple to think we live in a palace. I gave her the choice to have breakfast either in her room or in the family dining room. You had better get used to her. Believe me, she will be invaluable.

"The Lincoln Room is quite wonderful. Did you know that the sofa, three matching chairs, two slipper chairs, and four cabinet chairs are all from his 1860s Administration? Even the bathroom is cool. It has pale green opaque glass tiles and a mirrored dome ceiling light. The huge tub has a regal sandblasted etching of an American eagle. She will be provided with the same thick white towels and Aveda hair products we provide to all our honored guests. I want her to be overwhelmed by her surroundings. She will then be very supportive in her writings. The best way to turn a liberal journalist is to make them rich and give them inside information. Excuse me, now I must prepare for my meeting.

"Jboo, Itch, please sit down and have some spiked cider. Care for some ham and artichoke hearts? How about some peanut butter and jelly sandwiches and chocolate milk? I asked you here because we are going to push a bill through Congress, and you are the best men for the job. I was with that reporter. I know you are familiar with her work, Foxxy Hart, and for obvious reasons it made me think of stimulation. That made me think of a neat stimulus package we can sell to the American sheeple....erm....I mean *present* to the American sheeple.

"Jboo, most people think that the idea of trickle-down economics started with Ronald Reagan, specifically David Stockman, who was Reagan's budget director. The original term is supposed to be a creation of Will Rogers, who coined it during the Great Depression, but I was not there to hear him, so I really could not say if it is true or not.

"As far as I am concerned, that marvelous economic miracle was invented by you, Jboo, on that great day when you met your wife. You collided, and those rotten slimy eggs trickled down your legs. You have pioneered and championed supply-side economics from that day on. Six months ago, you suggested we release four billion dollars to four major corporations to test your theory. I am here to tell you tell you that it worked beyond your wildest dreams. That is why I want to take this to the next level, and appropriate twenty billion dollars for the next phase.

"This is what happened. The money was given equally to Lockness Marin, Standard Electric, Hallitosis, and Brownwater. In six short months that money was invested by those companies to grow the economy. Karl Krotch collected the data and made this spreadsheet. As you see, each company is listed separately. I did this to create a little competition between them. But what you will find most interesting is the grand total of all four companies at the bottom of the page.

As a direct result of the four billion dollar stimulus package, the following jobs were created:

7 janitorial-assistant positions
5 dishwasher's helpers
9 copier cleaners and paper loaders

11 telephone answerers
4 carpet dusters
2 paperclip dispensers
8 lunch wagon pushers
6 secretarial under-assistants
24 temporary loading-dock sweepers

That is seventy-six citizens who have been brought in off the street and given jobs, and except for the twenty-four temporary workers, they now have hospitalization, if they can afford the cab fare to the emergency room. I am going to give this info to Foxxy so she can leak it to FLOX News.

"Well done, Jboo."

# 37

"**R**hoda, we need a new distraction. We have unemployment rising, gas prices rising, food prices rising, and Medicare and Social Security benefits will not be raised to cover inflation.

"I am concerned. In the past all we needed was reality TV shows like *Ultimate Warrior, Dancing With the Degenerates*, or *New Jersey Voyeur*. I fear the sheeple are more restless than usual. Ralph in the CIA tells me there is an increase in Internet chatter. The NSA is monitoring random emails. As you know, they have specialized software that can be instantly programmed to recognize key words. They randomly checked twenty million communications, searching for words like food stamps, gas, Social Security, credit card payments, and then graphed the trends. My Security Council, Percy, and I are the only ones authorized to study the data. Not even the NSA people collecting it are aware of the results.

"No doubt about it, the sheeple are restless. I will eventually eliminate free universal Internet access. Instituting expensive subscriptions will cut down on traffic. But until that happens, all this back and forth chatter is annoying the shit out of me.

"This is what I would like to do until we can eliminate groups like MoveOver, The Daily Kos, and Huffington Post from mobilizing the un-American no-goods. We are going to beat them at their own game. We are also going to use the Internet, but instead of showing unauthorized photos of our much-maligned police roughing up a few minority criminals who deserve to be roughed up, we are going to give them cake and cookies to distract them.

"Rhoda, you were telling me that your ex used to beat you every Super Bowl Sunday if his team lost. That is one of the reasons you divorced him. If I remember correctly, he always bet on the losing team, you poor thing. But without knowing it, you provided a service for your country. You helped channel your husband's violence away from political mischief to just beating the shit out of you, which, as far as I am concerned, was not nearly as bad. So I would like to thank you for helping to protect this administration.

"That is why our lawmakers are working hand in hand with the corporations that control the media. We need a constant supply of athletic events, reality TV shows, shots of starlets who display their crotches as they get in and out of their limos, to distract the populace. We have direct control over who does or does not have their wardrobe malfunctions spread all over the country's computer screens. The starlets' spin-doctors kill each other for the space. Our Republican lawmakers get some neat vacation perks from the major news services as a result. We pre-empt international news to show these malfunctions. But unfortunately, they have become boring and predictable.

"Social unrest is rising in spite of the usual sops, so we need to create a new diversion. The sheeple want to feel they are a part of running this country. The morons have already been deluded into thinking that their vote counts. However, those with brains are staying home, not voting for either party, and are getting on their computers to make trouble. Those are the people we have to control.

"Here is how we are going to do it. We are going to create a new national agency called Pride in America. Every month we will ask the sheeple to contribute the names of their favorite things. There will be ten categories. As you know, there are unofficial favorites that have always represented our country. Our national bird is the bald eagle. We really have two songs, our national anthem, and 'God Bless America.' I can't stand it that the latter was written by a foreigner, but what are you going to do? But what is our favorite food, what is our favorite animal? We are going to ask the sheeple to vote on what they think our favorite symbols should be. Ten winners will be chosen each month and each given $10,000. That is $100,000 per month, and $1,200,000 per year. The money will be the big draw. The damn fools have about as much chance of being selected as they do of winning the lottery, but that will not stop them. I cannot think of a cheaper way to dumb down the sheeple.

"So without further ado, we will ask what is their favorite:
Singer
Song
Male athlete
Female athlete
Flower
Food
Drug
Alcohol
R-rated movie
Porn star

"We will announce the winners on the first day of the following month, and publish their photos and a short bio about them and their families. I will interview some winners on my monthly call-in show.

"The servers will be clogged with sheeple sending in their entries to Pride in America. They will no longer give a shit about lousy interest rates and no jobs."

# 38

"So, Rhoda, hooray! Finally! Justice Ginsmann is going to retire. It is way past time. I know you are interested in American history, especially my interpretation of it, so I will tell you why this is so important. We have had some great men on the court. Their photographs are right there on the South Wall of this very room. Their names are Justices Pierce Butler, James Clark McReynolds, George Sutherland, and Willis Van Devanter. In the 1930s, the New Deal pinkos called them the Four Horsemen of the Apocalypse, because they were the only jurors who had the courage to oppose FDR's giveaway programs, as he tried to turn us into the Socialist States of America. They were successful for a time, but then Van Devanter retired, and FDR put another pinko, Hugo Black, in his place. Then the balance of power shifted and the pinkos were in the majority.

"Ever since that appointment, the hard-earned money from those who built this country has been blatantly stolen by excess taxes, and redistributed to the sheeple in the form of Social Security, Medicare, and contributions to PBS. We already have a majority on the court of our kind of people, thanks to our Republican forebears. They chose strong, unwavering men like Antibody Scalia and Clarabell Thomas to lead the way. This is our chance to retain power long after we leave office. As you know, a seat on the Supreme Court is a lifetime appointment that cannot be challenged by the Democrats. We have a majority in both houses, so we can nominate anyone we choose. With six conservative justices, we can strike down Roe v Wade, put prayer back in our schools, disenfranchise all the affirmative action cases, scrap equal work for equal pay, make abortion universally illegal, and make it a crime to question the police. And that is only the beginning.

"Can you not get a whiff of the sweet smell of Utopia in the air? Our goal is to push the middle-class sheeple so low that they have to look up to see down."

"But Mr. President, aren't you afraid that you will ruffle a lot of feathers in the media if you nominate someone too radical?"

"Rhoda, I can see that you have really learned a great deal in the short time you have been my....erm....chief of staff. You are absolutely correct. We always want to stay at least two steps ahead of the other side. I always ask myself, what will Senator Bitch Sandcastle say? Then I steal her thunder by shutting her up even before she gets a chance to speak. Can you guess who I am going to nominate?"

"Sarah Lapin?"

"Nope, she would not understand the statues or the legal precedents, although she would look good with her robe pulled up."

"How about the first lady? She has a great legal mind."

"Oh, can you see that? Nora sitting on the bench? She also has a great *body*, and it would be a shame to hide that body under a robe, unless it's a see-through-mini version with red sequin trim. No, I have got my candidate. It is Senator Joe Liebestraum. Even though he is Jewish, he is more conservative than I am. All the liberals cannot say shit and they cannot accuse me of prejudice. We may make a few towelheads mad, but look in my left eye and see if I give a fuck."

# 39

# Eliminating Republican Bedbugs

## Bedbug removal

Republican bedbugs have become a real problem, especially in southern and midwestern states. No living environment is safe from their intrusion. They infect condos, apartments, homes, hotels, even RVs used by people on vacation. Those hit hardest are the poor and middle classes. Professional pest control, though effective, is very expensive. We show you some tried and true methods to get rid of these pests.

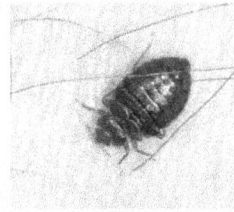

**GOP bedbug**

Pesticides alone will not eliminate bedbugs. You must also safeguard your home from future door-to-door campaigns. Most people are unaware that they have brought bedbugs into their homes. They can hide most anywhere. Republican bedbugs like to hide in your wallet, your medicine cabinet, and wherever you store your tea. The closet where you keep your purse and checkbook is especially vulnerable. Don't wait too long to begin treatment, because they multiply like crazy. While you sit in your car they can crawl inside your shirt, and you will inadvertently give one of them a ride to another neighborhood or your friend's house.

**Important fact to remember: All Republican bedbugs are blood suckers! They may try to convince you that they are not harmful, but do not believe them!**

- ☐ **Bedbugs won't bother you if you're awake and aware of your surroundings.**
- ☐ **Do not watch FLOX News on your bedroom television. They are attracted to empty-headed noise.**
- ☐ **Sleep with the light on. Republican bedbugs work best in total darkness.**
- ☐ **You cannot eliminate bedbugs by requesting a Catholic exorcism. They are much worse than the Devil.**

# Tried and true
# Republican bedbug
# removal solutions

Strip the bed, vacuum the mattress and box springs,
and enclose the mattress in a bedbug-proof encasement.
Empty out all dresser and nightstand drawers, and use
Diatomaceous earth (DE) dust for Republican control.
They will shrivel up and dry out when they come in
contact with DE, or any sound political logic.
For people in Red states with Tea Party Republican
bedbugs, you must triple the recommended dosage, and
apply it for five times longer than recommended.

# Start a Neighborhood
# Bedbug Awareness Group

Many of your neighbors may not be aware that they have
Republican bedbugs. If one house is infected, the chances
are that the dwellings to the left and right will also be
infected. If you live in a condo or apartment, the people
above and below you will have the same problem.

Republican bedbugs spread faster than liquid shit. Start
a support group on your block. Tell your neighbors not
to be embarrassed if they invited one of them into their
homes. These vermin often hide in the pages of

campaign literature.  They can be very persuasive when asking for votes, but  sooner or later they always wind up in your wallet.

# The absolute best way to eliminate Republican bedbugs

If all other treatments fail to get rid of these pests, there is one thing that *never* fails.  Turn your television to a news station and find an Elizabeth Warren interview.  Turn up the volume as loud as you can stand it.  This should send the little fuckers scampering out of your life for good.

Do not collect your live bedbugs and send them to the Republican Speaker of the House or the Republican Senate Majority Leader.  They won't kill them, out of professional courtesy.

"Rhoda!"

# 40

"Thank you very much. Mr. Speaker, Vice President Floy, members of Congress, distinguished guests, and fellow citizens, I have the dubious honor of delivering the State of the Union Address later than any president in history. I have waited so long because I wanted to make damn sure I had something important to say, rather than blab the usual shit that you have heard shoveled by my predecessors. Their speeches were handed to them by spin doctors, staff writers, and their political handlers. I want you to know that all these words and ideas are my own. Well, mine and Nora's. Actually, mostly Nora's, but it was up to me to make the final decision on what I would or would not say. Well, for the most part it was my final decision, but not necessarily entirely *my* final decision.

"As we gather tonight, our nation is fighting three wars, our economy is in a recessive tailspin, our environment is being despoiled, food and medical costs are skyrocketing, the civilized world faces unprecedented dangers from terrorists, hypnotists, philanthropists, optometrists, and multi-sexual trysts. However, I want to assure the American sheeple....erm....subjects, that the State of our Union has never been stronger.

"The American flag once again flies proudly over Dearborn, Michigan. However, the towelheads continue to razz us for being the Great Satan. In Arabland they have developed anthrax, nerve gas, nuclear weapons, biological weapons, cosmic death rays, and most important, weapons of mass destruction. They have kicked out our weapons inspectors, as well as our women's wrestling team. They are trying to hide their dastardly deeds from all of us. I will not rest until I find those weapons of mass destruction. Somewhere in Arabland, some sheik, in some hidden and forgotten sand dune, has squirreled away enough toxic shit to poison all the air and water in America. You and I cannot let that happen.

"This Axis of Evil will stop at nothing to steal our precious bodily fluids. They will poison our Yodels, Ring Dings, and Devil Dogs. I have asked my friends in the Pentagon to put up a defensive line of Patriot missiles around every brewery in America. There are some things that nobody, and I mean nobody, is going to fuck with.

"On the strictly domestic front, we have made great strides in putting America back to work. Mrs. Essy Tool is with us tonight. Essy's son Nomad had been out of work for eleven years. With our new stimulus program, he was able to find a temporary, assistant-loading-dock-sweeper's position with Standard Electric. They are both here in the audience. Essy and Nomad, will you please stand up and wave to all of America. (sustained applause)

"Thank you. Thank you. (waits for applause to die down) In the coming months, Congress and I will work together for productive hemp farms (applause) – cleaner oil pipeline spills (applause) – a broad-based internship program, for women only, ha ha (applause) – and a threefold increase in the size of the navels in our oranges (sustained applause). As you know, the prolonged drought in California has shriveled up the poor oranges so they look more like raisins. But we will not be defeated, not even by God! With my leadership, we took those shriveled navel oranges, and one by one, injected real fluid into them with syringes and orange juice imported from China. So once again, when you walk into your favorite supermarket, you will see the fruits of our labor. (applause)

"My fellow and gal-pal Americans, everything has a beginning. You know the old question: Which came first, the chicken or the egg? Well, it had to be the chicken, who else could have laid the egg? I do not know where the chicken came from, and that really is not the point. Great jobs start with great schools. In order to have a talented workforce, we must provide the bedrock foundation for our children to learn the skills necessary to function in our highly competitive, technologically-oriented world. To further this end, I am instituting a new education policy called *No Behind Left in the Child*. Our children are too fat. They need to cut down on vegetables and fruit. How can we expect them to think, when all their bodily energy is flowing down into their bottoms? *No Behind Left in the Child* will insist on high test scores. If a school does not meet our criteria and standards, I will instruct the federal government to close that school, turn it into a munitions factory, and force the students and teachers to make 30 mm shells for our Gatling guns.

"As president, one of my most important jobs is setting our priorities. We have languished far too long in La La Land, not knowing what our real place is on this Earth. I am here to tell all of you that our place is the righteous place, it is the only place, it is the only righteous place! (thunderous applause)

"As a great American once said, 'Ask not what I can do to you, ask what you have done to me, what I could have done to you, and what we should have done to each other.' It is in this spirit that I am going to create the New WPA. The New WPA will answer America's call for repaired roads and bridges, aqueducts to carry water for navel oranges, swimming pools for Republican congressmen, and labor for new prisons and detention centers throughout the land. I am asking Congress to reinstitute the draft for all Americans, not just those of military service age. I want each and every American to devote at least five years of service to our nation. Think of the future we can build with your hard work and my direction!

"In closing, I want to thank my wife Nora for her unselfish guidance and gentleness, my children Petunia and Alfonso for their obedient, sweet dispositions and unconditional support, and for the special guest now staying in our White House, who has shown me more positions than I ever dreamed possible.

"There is still time to watch the second half of *Dancing With the Degenerates*, so why do you not switch the channel? Oh, and God Bless America."

# 41

"**R**hoda, how did this happen? I *thought* the bed was much harder than usual to fold out. Something must be wrong with the springs, and it has snapped back into the couch position."

"Ow! There is another problem, Mr. President, we're trapped inside it."

"Wait, let me use my feet to push it. We will both push at the same time. Ready, set, push! Nothing, it will not budge. Can you crawl out on your side?"

"No, I can't move my feet. Maybe if you give me a push. Go ahead. Ow! No, that didn't help, I still can't move. What are we going to do?"

"Okay Rhoda, we will have to try harder. When I count to three we will use all our strength and push the springs back. Ready? One, two, three, push!"

"Mr. President, the couch is now on its back and our feet are up in the air, but we're still stuck inside. Is this sabotage? It doesn't seem natural."

"Shit, the staff will be here in ten minutes with the morning papers and breakfast. Okay, let me think. I am president for a reason. I can handle crisis in a calm manner and arrive at solutions that will save the day. Let me see...."

"Have you thought of anything yet? We have about five minutes left."

"Shut up, you stupid bitch! How the hell can I think with you talking all the time? We can move our arms. Move your blanket. Now I can see the label. What does it say underneath the locking instructions? I cannot read them without my glasses."

"Made in China."

"Fuck! Who do you have on duty this morning?

"Lucy is going to bring us breakfast and papers, but oh my, I forgot to tell you something, Mr. President, and I think you're going to be angry."

"What the hell else could you possibly tell me that would make me any angrier than I am?"

"Senator Sandcastle asked me if she could stop in right after breakfast, but she didn't say why."

"Fuck! And you agreed? You actually said, sure Bitchface, stop on by? I do not have to ask my boss, who hates everything about you? You moron, you said yes without consulting me? Oh stop crying, that is not going to help anything. Let me see, what can we do? The people who come into the room can see in through the sides of the sofa. Can you wrap that cover around yourself, since you are completely naked? Can you try to look like a stack of blankets? Can you reach your cellphone? Wait, I can reach mine! We do not have much time. Who should we call to get us out of this mess? Wait. There is only one person I can trust to not blab it all around the Capitol. I will call Percy. Damn! Damn! I got his message center. 'Vice President Percy Floy is not available to take your fucking call.' Pick up, you imbecile!"

"Mr. President, when you threw your phone it slid off the sheets, and I heard it bounce on the floor. It's now out of reach. What are we going to do? I hear footsteps coming down the hall, and it's more than one person. Senator Sandcastle must be with Lucy."

"This is what we are going to do. Sometimes confusion is the only way to gain the upper hand. When people see something they think is real and true, such as you and me in bed, all you can do is try to plant doubt by changing the nature of things and making the scene abstract. So, when that door opens, I want us to sing a song at the top of our lungs. What songs do you know?"

"How about Snotty Droopy Dingo Doggy, Ajax, The Cartwheels, or Foam at the Mouth. Do you know any songs from those groups, Mr. President?"

"Fuck no. How about the Beatles, the Rolling Stones, U2, or Elton John?"

"Sorry, Mr. President, they're before my time. How about the Marine Corps anthem? But why exactly are we singing?"

"We are going to tell them that we have formed a theatrical music group for senators, representatives, their staff members, and all White House personnel, and we are rehearsing one of the scenes. We will then ask them if they want to join in.

"Here they come, are you ready?"

"From the halls of Montezuma to the shores of Tripoli,
we will fight our country's battles
on the land and on the sea.
First to fight for right and freedom,
and to keep our honor clean...."

# 42

"**M**r. President, Ms. Dendron, Senator Sandcastle, and the rest of you, please do not leave this room. We have an intruder alert somewhere in the White House, and you are to remain here until they are found. It's best if you put your clothes on, sir, in the event we have to move you quickly to a safer location. I'm leaving five agents with you for increased security in case they are needed. Please don't be upset at all their military equipment, it's just a precaution. Please excuse me, I must coordinate our search."

"Just a moment, Agent Crawdad, I insist on knowing the nature of this intrusion. Is it one person, is it several, how did they get past security? I want answers."

"Yes sir, I do not yet know the answers to your questions, but I will find out."

"Is there any way this could have been prevented? What protocols have been breached?"

"I don't know yet, Mr. President, that's why I must leave you to find out."

"Agent Crawdad, what can the Secret Service do to prevent future intrusions?"

"I do not yet know, sir. I must leave you to determine the exact nature of the intrusion before I can propose any solutions."

"Do you believe these intruders to be armed? Do they have chemical weapons?"

"I do not know the nature of their armaments, if indeed any are present, sir."

"Why have you not left to do your job?"

"Yes sir, Mr. President, I'm on my way."

"One more thing, Agent Crawdad. Are the men you have guarding us aware of the nature of the threat?"

"No sir, they are not. But they are trained to attack whoever walks unannounced into this room."

"The first lady and my daughter Petunia are scheduled to visit this morning."

"It's best if they don't, sir. My men can get very jumpy. There's something about the corridors of power that increases the pressure on their trigger fingers."

"Well, Mr. President, I think it's great that we can put our differences aside long enough to cooperate on staging a musical. *The King and I* is a wonderful choice. I'll have Jennifer audition for Anna; she would love to annoy the king. I wonder how long we will have to wait before we have some news."

"It should not be too long. For Christ's sake, the White House is not as big as all that. What did you want to see me about, senator?"

"I would like to propose a moratorium on attack ads that are leaked through the media."

"Your timing is suspect, senator. After you leaked the piece about Republican bedbugs, now you want a moratorium before we can retaliate. I will think about it after I issue our rebuttal."

"Everybody on the ground, get on the ground! Now! Now!"

The Secret Service agents are shouting all at once. At that moment, nine intruders burst into the Oval Office.

"Agent Crawdad, what is your explanation of the events that have just transpired? I do not want any bullshit. I do not want any theories. I do not want any opinions. I just want facts. Is that understood?"

"Yes, sir. Here's what happened. The intruders did not know about the metal detectors, and the agent was distracted because one of them asked him where the bathroom was. While he was directing this person, the others walked right through the detector. It was very skillfully done. As you know, the detector is supposed to automatically shut down to prevent the next person from walking through unless the agent resets it. But somehow they jammed it. It malfunctioned and all the intruders walked through undetected. They went unnoticed until the unit came back online ten minutes later. They were able to penetrate through all areas, and that's how they wound up in the Oval Office."

"Who are they and where are they from?"

"Brownie Troop 147 from Muskogee, Oklahoma, sir."

# 43

"**G**ood morning. I called this special cabinet meeting for an important reason. We will not be continuing our agenda from last time, nor will anyone be allowed to introduce new material. Most of you don't know Bart Bassa from NSA. It was he who convinced me to call this session. Bart is in charge of compiling and storing all government email data. Much of the information we will be hearing about was gathered without the senders' or receivers' knowledge. I have seen some of this material, and believe me, its potential impact cannot be ignored.

"I am going to give the floor to Bart. Please tell everyone in the room why this is so important."

"Thank you, President Hades, and good morning to all. As you know, the Freedom of Information Act allows our lawmakers to access data that was never before available. Senator Bernice Sandcastle has requested emails from four cabinet members in this room as well as from other administration sources. I want you to be aware of what is on record in the event that you have to defend yourselves from possible allegations."

"We really appreciate that, Bart, and welcome to our team. But are we not protected for national security reasons? How can Sandcastle possibly have the right to access data that could betray vital, sensitive information?"

"There is a gray area here, Mr. President. The definition of *sensitive information* is open to interpretation. My boss may have a different opinion on what is or is not secret than would you or I."

"Who is your boss, Bart?"

"Samantha Sandcastle. She is the senator's sister."

"Fuck! Not another one! They are like omnipresent fungi, sickly green moss that sticks to wet surfaces and builds up between your toes. Too bad we can't spray them with disinfectant to make them disappear. Okay, Bart, what has NSA got?"

"We did have seven emails between you, Mr. President, and Foxxy Hart. You were discussing leaks. The messages are no longer a problem, because I successfully deleted them without Sandcastle's knowledge."

"Excellent work, Bart. Your performance may earn you a seat on this cabinet. What else is going on?"

"We have 114 emails from Percy Floy to Ludmila Kasyanenko and Natalia Bulgakov. In most of them, Mr. Vice President, you talk about launching your missile.

"We have nine emails from Ludwig Peckeroff to a woman named Flossie Filbert. Mr. Secretary, you speak of the Big Bang Theory, and you weren't talking about the formation of the universe. You also wrote to her about how big your shotgun is and that you're very glad she lets you bring it to bed. We also have nineteen emails between Secretary Peckeroff and Sarah Lapin about buckshot, and several discussions about her chopper's launching pad.

"We have forty-nine emails between Rhoda Dendron and Wayne Lapoopierre. There are graphic discussions about explosions, discharges, and reloading."

"Rhoda, you slut! So this is going on behind my back! Lapoopierre, you are no longer a part of this cabinet. This is getting very interesting. What else have you got, Bart?"

"We have 2,418 emails back and forth between Itch McCringell and the South Washington Sexual Experimentation Boutique. I believe they are the third largest contributor to your campaign, Senator McCringell. The text communications aren't good, but the photographs are much, much worse.

"We have 247 emails coming from inside the White House, but we're not sure of the source. The unknown sender has initiated a dialogue with male members of all four branches of our armed services. We've used our keyword recovery system and catalogued the terms most used. He or she writes a great deal about infiltration, strategic withdrawal, unauthorized entry, frontal attacks, amphibious landing, early warning, joint deployment, navel maneuvers, and target acquisition. It could be a direct threat, sir."

"Oh, that is just great! Is there any clue to who this person might be?"

"There is a signature on three of the emails, sir. Red Sequin."

# 44

"**M**r. President?"

"Yes, Slut-Face? What do you want? Oh, stop crying! You are still chief of staff, but Foxxy Hart is now my press secretary. Get over it. All good things must come to an end, and looks like we have had our day on the couch. We must move on. From this time forward, we will keep our relationship on a strictly professional level. What have you got for me?"

"Boo hoo. The president of the Unified Arab Protectorates has been invited by the Democrats to speak before a joint session of Congress next Thursday. I just thought you would want to know."

"Thank you, Rhoda. Please get me the vice president right away.

"Percy, you have got to be kidding. How did this happen?"

"It seems that 124 democratic senators and congressmen issued an invitation to Grand Sultan Prince Demented without consulting either you or me. Since the news has spread all over the world, we can't rescind the offer without angering our most important ally in the region."

"They *were* our most important ally until we learned that South West Sahara has three times as much oil as the UAP. Now they are just a nuisance. We are going to throw that opportunist to the sharks.    Sultan  Prince  Demented  is  up  for  reelection, reappointment,  re-installment,  reinsertion,  or  whatever  those primitive sheeple do over there.  That is the only reason he wants to come here, for a grand publicity stunt.  Percy, this is what I want us to do.  I want every Republican senator and congressman to show up for the address.  As soon as he speaks his first sentence, you all walk out.  At that moment, we will also turn off his microphone and the house lights."

"As vice president, aren't I supposed to remain at the podium?"

"Not only do you walk out, Percy, but you lead everyone else out. Is that clear?  Bring a powerful flashlight.   He will lose his election, and so will the Democrats lose the next presidential election.   They thought they were bypassing and dissing this administration, but all they did is shoot themselves in their respective foots.  Do you not just love it when the opposition party self-destructs?   We are going to investigate prosecuting the Democratic leadership for treason.  I love House cleaning.

"Speaking of house and chamber cleaning, how is the renovation progressing?  We have needed new Senate seating for fifty years."

"Very well, Nick.  Crug Picknose of Brownwater has a great idea. We all wanted custom carved seats made of rare Brazilian rosewood.  As you know, there is a ban on importing that beautiful wood.  But Crug pulled strings to us get all we needed. We sent them some of the usual bartering items:  jet fighters, missiles, and 250,000 head restraints.   What's a few thousand Amazon rainforest acres more or less?  The only thing he wants in return, and I think it's a very doable small thing, is for us to place an inlaid plaque on each chair with the Brownwater logo.  They will pay for the installation, which will save the taxpayers eight thousand dollars per chair."

"Excellent idea. Let us do the same thing with the chairs in the House and Supreme Court. Contact Mary Ellen Nonsense of Lockness Marin; Junco Inman, of Standard Electric; and Dribble J. Lesser of Hallitosis, and ask them to donate money for new podiums and gallery seating. Naturally they can also have their logos inlaid into the furniture. This is the kind of government/industry partnership that I have always dreamed about."

# 45

"**H**ere is something you did not know. I keep a diary. Most of the time I write entries at my bedroom desk, about an hour before I climb into bed to watch a movie. Sometimes I do what I am doing now. I get out of bed and come to the Oval Office at three a.m. I do this when I have something on my mind, or when I need to recap events and put things in perspective. I generally talk out loud before I write anything down, and it is usually exactly as spoken. After all, writing is just speaking on paper. The office is dark except for my desk lamp with a green shade. You have probably seen these, except that mine has a sterling silver base and was made at Tiffany.

"This is not a high point in my life. Spineless Percy did not leave the podium like we agreed to lead the Republicans out of the chamber during Prince Demented's address. Only fifteen brave members of my party had the courage to turn their backs on that towelhead. If Percy thinks he will be on my ticket in the next election, he is totally delusional. I am going to brainstorm a way of replacing him immediately. If I can get Vice President Grouse to resign, I can remove Floy just as easily.

"My son Alfonso does nothing but play video games. He cannot name three members of the Supreme Court. My daughter Petunia has made friends with the White House janitorial and maintenance staff. They sneak down to the boiler room and smoke weed. Who the hell knows what else they are doing down there? My wife Nora seems to be screwing most of the members of our armed forces. My chief of staff, Rhoda, has been carrying on with Lapoopierre behind my back. My approval rating in the polls has slipped to below 17 percent, which is a new all-time low for a sitting president. The Sandcastle Bitchfaces are conspiring to publicize my cabinet's private emails.

"If you think I am going to whine and hide in the corner, you are sadly mistaken. That is why I am sitting here alone in the Oval Office writing to Whomeverthefuck will wind up reading this diary. The best way to formulate strategy is to verbalize it. I have to get the ideas from my brain into my mouth before they can become the law of the land. It seems like a simple enough process. At least it has always worked for me.

"Do you know what really helps? I have a miniature pinball game. It launches a tiny red metal ball. There are five balls in a row at the bottom of the glass. The goal is to get the highest score by evading the holes and hazards throughout. After launching the ball, you get to spin one wheel on either side to control the hazards. The whole game is only seven inches wide by one foot long. A perfect score is 500, but even the best players hardly ever get above 400. On some nights I can get close to 450. Tonight I got 465, so I know I can make good decisions for America.

"The first thing I am going to do is make Bart Bassa from NSA the head of Homeland Security. That will make him Samantha Sandcastle's boss: end of email problem. I have a new press secretary, Foxxy Hart. So far she is working out fine.

"I know exactly what to do about my approval ratings, and the congressional rebellion that seems to be stirring. Way back in 2004, just before the presidential elections, George W. Bush raised the nationwide terrorist alert six times to orange. Let me tell you about alerts. They come in many pretty colors. Green is for low risk of terrorists attacks, blue is for general risk, yellow is for significant risk, orange is for high risk, and red is for severe risk of attack. Bush was smart enough not to go to red, because when nothing happened, the sheeple would have accused him of crying wolf. Even then, Homeland Security Chief Tom Ridge wondered why the White House wanted to issue so many orange alerts.

"Duh, the answer is so simple. Here was a mastermind at work. This was right after 9/11, and Americans were scared shitless that the same thing would happen again. The sheeple did not want to be toasted in their own shopping malls, so they voted for the one person who could 'keep them safe'. Bush and Cheney were experts in Terror Management Theory (look it up in The Google) and used those principles to control the sheeple.

"That is exactly what I am going to do now. We have three active terrorist groups that are causing trouble around the world. I will get Bart Bassa to issue the first of my orange alerts. I will have our agents find and remove plastic explosives from the fourteenth hole of the U.S. Open Golf Championships at the Congressional Country Club, Blue Course, in Bethesda. This will be during prime time, with the entire country watching.

"I will give a news conference introduced by a highly agitated and forceful Foxxy Hart, to tell the American sheeple that we must be prepared. Since we found explosives in the fourteenth hole at the Open, and we do not know where else the enemy will plant them, I must raise an orange alert.

"I will have stirring footage of our armed forces and police guarding airports, tennis clubs, supermarkets, and WalWart stores. The message is that any Main Street in the USA could be the next target, but we have got your back, America!  The more afraid the sheeple become, the higher my approval ratings will rise.  Watch them soar from 17 percent to 54 percent.  It will not take more than a few weeks."

# 46

"**W**elcome to *Greet the Press*. I'm Gnarly Schaefer. We have another first for *Greet the Press*. Since 1947 we have pioneered television journalism. Our very special guest this evening is the President of the United States, Nick Hades. We're honored, Mr. President, that you chose *Greet the Press* for your first live television interview. This promises to be an interesting show.

"Questioning the president tonight will be Harvey Schwartz from the *New York Times*, and Hymie Wart and Bill O'Hara from FLOX News. I must say, Mr. President, that our news show airs right after two unexpected announcements. You have raised the terrorist alert to orange, and you have recalled our ambassador to the Unified Arab Protectorates.

"Our regular viewers know our format, but perhaps we can deviate somewhat for this special interview. As moderator I usually smooth out the rough edges, switch topics if the discussion bogs down, and direct the flow of the show. I'm not going to do that this evening, but instead will take off my moderator's hat and join the members of the press who will be questioning the president. Each of us will have five minutes. When the red light goes on, the next interviewer may begin his questioning.

"I thought we should go in alphabetical order. So, Bill O'Hara is first, followed by me, then Harvey, who I barely beat out by Schaefer to Schwartz, and fourth will be Hymie Wart. Bill, the floor is yours."

"Thank you, Gnarly, and good evening, Mr. President. First of all, I must congratulate you for having the courage to fight terrorism wherever it rears its ugly head, and for putting the Unified Arab Protectorates on notice that they can't toy with our political system. I guess my first question is, when will you raise the alert to red? Does an attack have to be imminent? Who decides when, where, and how these alerts are broadcast?"

"Great question, Bill. I am the one who must make that difficult decision. I am the decider. I use all the knowledgeable resources at my command. I receive input 24/7 from Homeland Security, the CIA, the FBI, the NSA, U.S. Army and U.S. Navy Intelligence, and the NRA....erm....no, not the NRA, I was thinking about something else. Then I fabricate the evidence, I mean I decide if the evidence requires a military response. The level will go to red if more Silly Putty is found inside U.S. Open golf cups, for example. Did I say Silly Putty....erm....that is what my friends at Homeland Security call the stuff, you know, dark humor. Naturally, it is a highly advanced and dangerous formula of plastic explosive."

Red light.

"Mr. President, what proof do you have that terrorists planted the so-called Silly Putty at the U.S. Open? The only people who were seen in the area were golfers, caddies, and the gallery. Nobody was carrying anything except the caddies who had golf bags, women with purses, and many people with cameras. How could terrorists smuggle this past security and all the picture-takers? Where are the lab tests on the plastic explosives? Don't you feel you owe the American people an explanation of who may be responsible for this crime?"

"Mr. Schwartz, if we knew who did it, they would already be in jail. That is why I raised the terrorist alert to orange. The lab results are classified. Do you honestly think I will publicize the formula for other terrorists to copy? Do you not have any brains at all? If I knew who was responsible, damn it, I would already have squashed them like ugly bugs. My job is to protect America, not answer idiot questions from some wormboy who wants to placate every poor-assed crackpot dictator in the Third World."

Red light.

"Mr. President, was your pulling our ambassador from the UAP retaliation for the Democrats inviting him to speak before Congress? Aren't you afraid that the American people will see this as a lame, petty, political response, and reckless statesmanship?"

"Let me ask *you* something, Mr. Schaefer. If you look at your desktop computer, do you understand everything about it? Do you know how it works? What about the car you drove to this broadcast, or the jet plane you will ride in tomorrow? Do you know the science involved in these products? Do not bother answering, because the answer is no. You have no idea how your computer works. What makes you think that the affairs of state are any less complex than your computer? I must balance hundreds of items, weigh consequences that most people have no idea are involved. I must study causes and effects that even a hot-shot pinko journalist like you has no knowledge of. Before you accuse me of reckless statesmanship, look at yourself and all the other pinko journalists of this country asking reckless questions."

Red light.

"Mr. President, I'm disappointed in the vice president. I thought for certain that he would lead the Republican charge out of the joint session to censure Prince Demented. Are you upset with Floy? How can you gather the troops to fight for our cause?"

"Hymie, I have learned not to hold grudges. In a perfect world, of course I would have liked him to do as you just said. But we are not looking at a single event, or even one grand battle. Our triumph will be dozens of small battles, won by speaking the truth, launching progress, expanding our economy, raising our salary caps, and putting the citizens' hard-earned funds in the hands of the brave troops that you just mentioned. Together, freshly enriched and emboldened, and protected by Homeland Security, we will forge ahead!"

Red light.

# 47

# Eliminating Republican Termites

## Termite removal

Republican termites are eating away at the foundation of our country. Like Republican bedbugs, they are most active in our warmer states. Don't be fooled by the placid, tidy look of your home, the beauty of the siding, the well-kept green shrubbery and lawn. Underneath it all lurks Republican termites, ready to eat away your investment until there's nothing left. By the time you notice the damage, it will be too late to avoid costly repairs.

**GOP termites in caucus**

You haven't voted in years. They gerrymandered their way into your state and now see what has happened. Removal is extremely difficult because the termites themselves own the pest-control companies. You know, these are the same termites who refused to raise the minimum wage, while voting themselves huge pay increases and benefits.

Don't expect a quick fix. It took a long time for them to burrow underground and build their colonies. They feed on deadwood and can be found eating any available material. Getting rid of them will take a community effort, skill, cunning, and the right equipment for the job.

**Important fact to remember: All Republican termites are parasitic. They eat away the homes of hardworking people who built them. After they weaken your structure, they foreclose on your property.**

☐ **Sunlight will kill Republican termites.**
☐ **Use a magnifying glass to burn their leaders.**
☐ **Boric acid and PBS will kill them instantly by shutting down their nervous systems and dehydrating them.**
☐ **Democratic nematodes placed around your garden will kill termite larvae. Vote for them in the next election.**

☐ **Fannie Mae and Freddie Mac termites are especially difficult to regulate.**

# Be aware that Republican termite colonies have a network of outside support.

Subprime mortgage-lending infestor termites have bankrolled the colonies to the extent that they can move into your neighborhood unopposed.  They prey upon people who have overextended themselves due to bad loans.  After the infestor-sponsored termites have eaten away at our neighbors' homes, and your once prosperous friends have lost all their worldly possessions, they spawn other termite colonies to continually increase their profits at the expense of all the displaced families.

# What you should do if all do-it-yourself remedies fail to get rid of Republican termites

There is a time to call a professional.  Most of the chemicals used in termite removal are dangerous.  Electric shock treatments,  where they apply current directly to your walls, highly concentrated orange oil extracts, arsenic trioxide, and Permethrin dust can be highly poisonous.  These methods are best left to the professionals.

There is one pest-control person who isn't owned by the infestor termites.  I suggest you vote for her in the next election:   Elizabeth Warren, D – Mass.


"Foxxy!   Who will rid me of this meddlesome bitch?"

# 48

"**W**elcome to the Pariah Winfredo show. From May 6 to 12 we're celebrating Children's Book Week. This is the 98th year of the longest-running national literacy initiative in the country. When you teach a child to read and to have a love of books, she or he will make their whole lives richer. It will be a lifelong habit that will change them forever.

"We are honored today to have the first family with us. Nora Hades, the first lady, Petunia Hades, the first daughter, and Alfonso Hades, the first son, will be...."

"I'm not the first son, I'm the only son."

(Nervous laughter)

"Yes, the word 'first' is open to interpretation. Only a *reader* could tell you that it has many meanings. We will be discussing their favorite books, and how reading has changed their lives.

"Since you seem so eager, Alfonso, I'll start with you. What is your favorite book, not necessarily of all time, although that would also be interesting, but what are you reading now?"

"I have lots of favorites. *Call of Duty Black Ops II* is neat. I especially like books I can load on the screen. They are called 'movies.' Instead of stupid, useless words written in black ink on dead trees, they flash in front of my eyes right below the action. Late at night, when everyone is asleep, I turn on the captions. I've learned a lot of lower American slang and words from Latin American popular street culture from these games and movies."

"That is *very* interesting, Alfonso, but you really aren't reading a book when you play *Black Ops II*."

"What's a book?"

"We'll get back to you in a minute, Alfonso. Let's talk to your beeeautiful sister. Petunia, I see you have a gold book pin. Was that a gift, or did you buy it yourself?"

"Pariah, I've had it all my life. It belonged to my grandmother, bless her heart, who taught me to read while my mother was helping my father get elected Governor of Indiana. Her favorite books, and mine too by the way, are the novels of Jane Austen. They are so wholesome and uplifting. She knew a great deal about the false social graces and hypocrisy of 18th century England. There's no smoking weed, shooting up dope, oral sex, bestiality, sadomasochistic dalliances, torture, mass starvation, forced servitude, and demonic possession that there is in most of my other favorite books.

"From the time I was two years old, my mother instilled in me a love of virtual books. What is a book? It is words on paper. If you wrote down this conversation, and put it in book form you would have Pariah said this, and Petunia said that, then Pariah said this, and Petunia said that. Nobody buys sleeping pills anymore. All you need to do is pick up a good book, and wham, you're out like a light. That's why my other books are virtual books. They are all R, and X-rated videos.  I like it when words jump off the page and turn into sound and exciting images."

(Nervous laughter)

# 49

Greetings to all:

I'm Bernice Sandcastle, Independent Senator from Vermont.

I've made an interesting discovery. When we study the largest employers in all fifty states, an ugly fact appears, which I will tell you about.

But first, the good news. In all but one Blue state (states that voted decidedly Democratic in the last four presidential elections), the largest employers are different and varied. In my state the largest employer is the University of Vermont. In New Hampshire it's Dartmouth Hitchcock Medical Center. In Maine it's Hannaford Supermarkets. In Minnesota it's the Mayo Clinic. In California it's the UCLA Health System.

However, in twenty other states the largest employer is WalWart.

What does this mean? Well, let's look at the states where the Walmann family reigns supreme:

Alabama
Arizona
Arkansas
Florida
Georgia

Illinois
Kentucky
Louisiana
Mississippi
Montana
North Carolina
Ohio
Oklahoma
South Carolina
Tennessee
Texas
Virginia
West Virginia
Wyoming

I went back through the last four presidential elections. One of these states, Illinois, is decidedly a Blue state. *It is the only one.*

Three of the states, Florida, Ohio, and Virginia, voted twice for Republicans and twice for Democrats. So they are neither Red nor Blue. Let's call them neutral, or tossup states. My chief of staff and friend Jen calls them Purple states.

All the others are decidedly Red. There is only one Blue state of the twenty, and fourteen of the twenty states also have Republican governors.

The reason that WalWart is so successful in these Red states is because an exploitative environment has been created and nurtured by governors and greedy Republican state and national legislators. They don't care if hard-working people have adequate pay or proper medical benefits. They are anti-union, anti-

Affordable Health Care, and are against raising the minimum wage.

We have only to look at recent news to see the fight in Tennessee between Volkswagen's UAW and union-busting Governor Haslam. It's the same with Governor Walker in Wisconsin, who is in the process of dismantling his state's unions. It won't be long before WalWart can add that state to the list.

Let's take a look at some of America's richest exploiters:

| | |
|---|---|
| #4 Charles Krotch | 42.5 Billion |
| #4 David Krotch | 42.5 B (tie) |
| #6 C. Walmann | 41.1 B |
| #7 Jim Walmann | 39.7 B |
| #8 Alice Walmann | 38.5 B |
| #9 S. Robson Walmann | 38.1 B |

If the Walmann family were to give a mere 20 percent (31.48 billion dollars) of their net worth back to their employees, all of the workers would have a decent living wage, medical and retirement benefits for life, and be able to put their children through college.

The top 1 percent richest Americans own 34.6 of our net worth. The bottom 90 own 26.9 of our net worth.

What about our lawmakers?

| | |
|---|---|
| Rep. Darrell Issa (R-California) | 451.1 million |
| Rep. Jane Harman (D-California) | 435.4 million |
| Rep. Vern Buchanan (R-Florida) | 366.2 million |
| Sen. John Kerry (D-Massachusetts) | 295.9 million |

| | |
|---|---|
| Rep. Jared Polis (D-Colorado) | 285.1 million |
| Sen. Mark Warner (D-Virginia) | 283.1 million |
| Sen. Herb Kohl (D-Wisconsin) | 231.2 million |
| Rep. Michael McCaul (R-Texas) | 201.5 million |
| Sen. Jay Rockefeller (D-West Virginia) | 136.2 million |
| Sen. Dianne Feinstein (D-California) | 108.1 million |
| | |
| Combined net worth | 2.8 Billion dollars |

Notice that the so-called 'party of the people' has six of the ten richest lawmakers. The Hades family is worth almost a billion dollars. I'm sure Nora has had to cut back for appearances' sake. The first family can't publicly display the splendor they are used to basking in. All of the 435 members of the House and all 100 senators are multi-millionaires, except for me, of course. It makes sense that they won't put pressure on the Walmanns to increase wages and institute 100 percent medical benefits. Snakes don't make other snakes uncomfortable, due to professional courtesy.

There is a proverb, I think it's Turkish, that goes like this: 'Close your eyes to his countenance. Close your ears to his words. Watch his hands.' Those mealy-mouthed lawmakers have their hands in our pockets. That's why I'm an Independent.

The bottom line here is that if America continues to vote for the Republican party, which is far worse for the common man than are the Democrats, we will see the continued erosion of our hard-working middle class. Money will flow rapidly upward while more and more people sink into poverty and despair. By the time President Hades is through stealing from us, we will have devolved back into the feudal era of surfs and vassals.

It's so simple. Don't shop at WalWart. Don't vote for Republicans in the next election. (Oh, and throw out the rich Democrats as well.)

Thank you for everything you do for your families and your country.

Bernice Sandcastle
United States Senator – Vermont

# 50

"**A**ccording to the *New York Times*, in an article written by Harvey Schwartz, I quote, 'The Sandcastle Bill to rebuild our crumbling infrastructure was defeated in the Senate today by a vote that went strictly along party lines.' Now that is the kind of news I want to hear. It must have really chapped that liberal pinko's butt to have to pen that piece. Foxxy, there is no substitute for numbers.

"Who the hell cares about our infrastructure? As long as our airport runways are up to standard so we can use our private jets. Brooklyn Bridge comes tumbling down, tumbling down, tumbling down, Brooklyn Bridge comes tumbling down, on my fair lady Sandcastle's head.

"I wonder if it ever dawns on her that we have a *majority* in both houses. I am in *opposition* to her bill. Even if by some miracle she got it through Congress, my veto would have killed it deader than hell. Do you know what the stupid bitch tried to do? Listen to this, it is an absolute hoot. How did she propose to pay for all these roads and bridges? She tried to close the tax shelter loophole. She wanted to make it illegal for corporations and wealthy individuals to set up offshore accounts!

"Kapow! She shot herself in her foots. Every Republican in Congress has money in overseas tax shelters. She wants the 150 billion dollars per year returned to pay for her infrastructure improvements. As the late, great, Jackie Gleason once said, 'Har, har, hardy, har, har.' Who in their right mind is going to voluntarily bring their profits back into this country to be taxed? Would a bank robber, who got away clean and is enjoying his loot while basking on some South Sea island beach, come back into town, turn himself in, and get thrown into jail? Republicans are not masochists, we are sadists. Har, har, hardy, har, har! When is it going to dawn on these morons that it is useless to ask the police to police themselves? We do not vote ourselves congressional salary and benefit *decreases*. They do not know of the famous Hades loop. *We are in power because we have all the money. We get to keep all the money because we are in power.*

"I am so thankful for our wonderful banking friends in the Cayman Islands, Switzerland, Luxembourg, Bermuda, and the British Virgin Islands. Nora and I have 650 million stashed in the BVI. It is really neat to be able to conduct banking business and vacation in paradise at the same time. It would be just awful if our tax shelters were in Iceland, Greenland, the Sahara, or Newark.

"I must say that I am awestruck by our public relations spin doctors. We have totally convinced the sheeple that big government is bad. We have circulated photos of rugged individualists wearing tri-cornered patriot hats, holding muskets and flags with snakes that say 'don't tread on me' on them. They have bought it hook, line, and sinker, no net needed. It used to be a bit of a challenge to worm and weasel our way into power. Now it is just like shooting fish in a barrel.

"I love sheeple-shearing. Every time a right-wing Republican needs a new wool coat, he goes to the sheeple farm with his favorite high-speed electric shears and removes their wool. This wool gets spun into a fine tailored garment for the stalwart, superior, Republican, speculator-banker to protect him from the elements.

"Naturally the sheeple then have to stand out in the cold pasture without their wooly coats. You bet, Foxxy, it is all about numbers. The sheeple voted for the very individuals who are shearing the wool from their bodies. Are we good or what?"

# 51

"**W**e have soundly defeated the Sandcastle Infrastructure Bill. Now it is time to go on the offensive. I intend to be as offensive as possible. Itch, Jboo, care for some artichoke hearts, ham, peanut butter and jelly sandwiches? How about some spiked apple cider?

"Gentlemenses, we need an author. Let me explain what we are going to do. I have written a bill, but it would not be right for me to introduce it. It is not politic for me to sign something I have written. I want to appear as another independent voice in favor. Neither would it be politic for either of you to pen the measure. So, you are both to agree on the best author. Select some rising star in the Tea Party. I am merely the ghostwriter, and only the three of us and the soon-to-be-selected author will know the bill's true origin.

"I know both of you feel as I do, that we owe a great debt to those who have come before. With brilliant foresight, our Republican forebears created a fertile field in which to plant our new crop. The date was January 21, 2010. The place was the U.S. Supreme Court. After arguments that began in March of 2009, they passed the now landmark Citizen's United Decision. There is one sentence in that case that changed the course of history in our favor. The United States Supreme Court held that the First Amendment of our Constitution prohibits the government from restricting independent political expenditures by a nonprofit corporation. The principles argued by the court have also been rightfully extended to include for-profit corporations and other associations that we fondly know as PACS.

"In other words, gentlemenses, corporations have the right to free speech, and giving money, as determined by the court, is free speech.

"I would like to expand on this ruling. If corporations have the same rights as citizens, why limit those rights only to campaign contributions? I love history. I was looking at turn-of-the-twentieth-century photographs of mill towns in the Appalachian Mountains of the southern United States. Whole towns were built around those factories. The workers had shacks, most without indoor plumbing, constructed by the company. The workers were charged rent, but the companies made sure that the worker's wages covered the rent and basic food for survival. These foods were sold at the company store, of course, further expanding mill profits and ensuring the continued loyalty of the workforce. Shit, they did not have the money, health, or strength to go anyplace else. Do you remember the Tennessee Ernie Ford song, 'Sixteen Tons?' 'I owe my soul to the company store.' He got it right.

"You know about movie sequels. A sequel to *Star Wars* is called *Star Wars: The Force Awakens*. If they had not used the *Star Wars* name, there would not have been any resonance with the original movie. Since all that work has already been done for us by the Supreme Court, I feel it is only right to label our new bill Citizens United: The Force Awakens.

"There are 250 pages of proposals that we will pass through Congress and sign into law. Here are some of the high points:

A – Since corporations have the right to free speech, they also have the right to regulate the behavior of their employees. The Democratic model must be secondary to the rules of the corporation. The right for an individual to choose his manner of dress, for example, must be secondary to company rules. If the company dress code calls for a business suit and tie, the worker must dress as he is told to keep his job.

B – Corporations have the right to decide when and how a worker receives medical benefits, if they choose to pay them at all. When valued employees become ill, they should have nothing to worry about. Increasing the company bottom line will get the worker a much lower co-pay at the company clinic.

C – The corporation has the right to examine all portable device communications of its employees. For security reasons the CEO has the right to know what the workers are saying. This will include use of these devices when off company property. Disloyal employees will be immediately discharged.

D – Each corporation has the right, according to Citizens United: The Force Awakens, to decide which employees shall have vacation time, sick days, and pay raises. They will no longer be automatic, nor prescribed by law. Any attempts at government regulation will be against the U.S. Constitution, specifically the right to corporate free speech.

E – OSHA (Occupational, Safety, and Health Administration) rules will be privatized. For us to have a robust economy, it is up to the individual (I love that word) corporation to decide what safety measures are to be used. If these measures adversely impact the bottom line, The Force Awakens statues will allow the corporation to remove the safety measures.

"Gentlemenses, once again we are about to make history. There is nothing quite so satisfying as writing something today that will live long into tomorrow."

# 52

# Removing Republican Head Lice

## GOP head lice are spreading throughout America

Republican head lice have made a horrible comeback. They have developed resistance to many insecticides, logic, a spirit of cooperation, and can no longer be counted on for bi-partisan support. Sadly, they must be eliminated. "Smoke and mirrors" is a term used when they are trying to confuse you by obfuscating an issue. When studying people with GOP lice, things are seldom as they seem. For instance, a Republican woman sitting in a hotel room using her hair drier is not grooming herself. She is trying to rid herself of GOP head lice. When you hear news that a Republican congressman takes five showers per day, it isn't because he's extremely clean, it's because he's trying to rid

**GOP Lice At a Party**

his scalp of lice.

There are other tell-tale signs of infestation.

When you see Republicans grooming each other, specifically when they pick nits out of each other's hair and eat them, that's a sign that they aren't well. They learned this technique from observing Republican monkeys at their 1968 national convention. You don't want to share baseball caps with these people. You don't want to sit behind them in a crowded arena, especially if there's a headwind.

**GOP Senators Eating Nits In Hot Tub**

GOP head lice have become more resistant to insecticides in recent years, and killing the lice is only part of the battle. You must also kill their eggs. The old generation seems to have spawned a new generation with most of the old values. They can no longer be persuaded to leave office voluntarily; they must be thrown out. Here are some important facts that every freedom-loving Democrat must be aware of:

**GOP lice can live without breathing for over three hours. They will even survive under chlorinated pool water. The**

212

little fuckers are hard to kill. They also spread to other parts of the body and merge with Tea Party pubic lice and ultra-conservative armpit lice. When they are in total control, they will create one lousy body politic.

What should you do if a Republican louse invades your body?

☐ Obtain a specially designed louse comb, available through your Obamacare clinic.
☐ Use A-200 Pyrethrum spray.
☐ Olive oil causes them to suffocate and die.
☐ Apply the oil and wear a shower cap.
☐ Remember they can live without breathing for many hours, and without thinking for many weeks. (Best not to use the olive oil on your next pizza.)
☐ Use a hair drier on freshly washed hair to kill 85 percent of the nits.
☐ Attend a folk concert by Joan Baez or Bob Dylan. The music usually kills them.
☐ Whatever you do, never listen to O'Reilly or

# There is a last resort method of removal if all your efforts to purge these pests fail.

If all your work to dislodge GOP lice is unsuccessful, please don't despair.  Reconcile yourself to the fact that they can never be totally eliminated.  At best, they can be controlled.  The crucial word to use when describing them is "minority."

For your body and our country to be healthy, they must be in the minority.  Here's the group to turn to:  The National Association of Lice Treatment Professionals, formed in 2012 for people who need the absolute best nit-picking service.  Write to Senator Bernice Sandcastle – Independent, Vermont – for information that will help you to purge these vermin from your system.

"Foxxy!  Have you seen my comb?"

214

# 53

"Rhoda, let me know the minute Helena Handbasket arrives. She is the new chairman of the Republican National Committee, and we have some important business. I see that you and Foxxy have become quite friendly. This is good. Just make sure you are not plotting anything behind my back. I have a very large boot, and you would both find yourselves on the 'wrong side of the door,' as William Shakespeare once said.

"Hello Helena, please sit down. Care for some artichoke hearts, ham, peanut butter and jelly sandwiches, or some spiked apple cider? Congratulations on your new post. Chairman of the RNC is an extremely important position."

"Thank you, Mr. President, but I'm not Chairman of the RNC. I'm Chairperson of the RNC."

"Of course, of course, we must be politically correct. And we will not talk about history, after all that is *his* story. We will change it to *herstory*. We also will not discuss men and women. Do you want to know why? Because women have *men* in their name. Yup, it is *wo* to *men*. And we will not discuss *men*opause for the same reason. Believe me, Nora is going through the change, and it gives me pause to be anywhere near her. And let us not discuss women's health. Women can no longer have a hysterectomy. It is now a *her*sterectomy. My, my, we do have a lot of rewriting to do."

"Perhaps you are correct, Mr. President. However, there is no substitute for the word *dick*. What did you want to see me about?"

"Miss, excuse me, *Ms*. Handbasket, I would like to begin the process now of selecting my running mate for the next election. This is in strict confidence, but Percy Floy has not shown the kind of leadership I expected. Although the timing is not right at the moment, soon I will replace him with someone I want to share the ticket with. Rather than make this decision myself, which of course I have every right to do, I think it in the best interest of the party to include you in the decision."

"I'm honored that you would consider my recommendation. Your approval rating has jumped 19 percent since you instituted that orange alert. A few more such alerts and you will have the mandate you need to replace Floy. I always did feel that his relationship with those Russian twins was somewhat unnatural, and not in the best interests of the people. Who would you like to recommend?"

"Helena, let us go through the list. I will not summarize the good and bad points of each person. What I will show is the latest FLOX News polls showing their nationwide popularity. As far as I am concerned, numbers tell all. You cannot fool the FLOX polls.

"Let us start at the bottom. Here are the names and approval ratings:

| | |
|---|---|
| John Kasich | 1.7% |
| Rick Santorum | 1.8 |
| Bobby Jindal | 2.0 |
| Rick Perry | 3.0 |
| Ted Cruz | 4.6 |
| Marco Rubio | 5.0 |

| Chris Christie | 6.4 |
| Ron Paul | 8.4 |
| Mike Huckabee | 10.2 |
| Ben Carson | 10.6 |
| Scott Walker | 16.6 |
| Jeb Bush | 16.6 |

"86.9 percent. That's what you get when you add up the combined popularity ratings of all the candidates. Here is a fact you did not know. I asked my friends Karl and Adolph Krotch to conduct another poll. They added a new name to the mix and carefully and discreetly polled 5,000 key Americans across all social strata. This other name got 88.4 percent approval. When this person's name was included, Scott Walker's and Jeb Bush's rating dropped to under three percent, and she got a higher polling score than all the other candidates combined.

"That person is my wife, Nora Hades. She has this country in her red-sequined hip pocket. If I appoint her vice president, she will do a brilliant job in the Senate, and with her on my ticket in the next election, we cannot lose. There is a precedent here. Bill Clinton was president and Hillary Clinton is running for president."

"That may be true, sir, but they didn't run on the same ticket."

"That is a mere formality, Ms. Handbasket. I want Nora to be my vice president before she gets any ideas about running for president."

# 54

"The three of us know what, or should I say *whom*, we have in common. We all know he has a stretched-out Komodo Dragon tattoo on an ever-expanding stomach, and that he has been somewhat under-endowed. Madeleine, although you never had the 'pleasure' of bedding with the president, I'm sure you can appreciate what we're saying. Why are you blushing?"

"Nora, you have to include me in your group, a couple of times, that's all, but not since he got his new tattoo."

"Holy shit, are there any females he hasn't made a move on?"

"Bernice Sandcastle, because she would kick him so hard his gender would change."

"So, it's the four of us. I know you are wondering where we go next, so I'll get right to the point. My husband is worried about the upcoming presidential election. I can sense that he is going to ask me to be his running mate. I will smile politely and thank him for his wonderful vote of confidence. While all that is going on, and he sits in his easy chair of false security, we will be preparing to snatch the office out from under him.

"Madeleine, you are going to be Secretary of State in my new administration. We have agreed that you are no longer working for Bernice. You know, you never mention your past. There is more to your history than chopping onions. I've learned that during the Gulf War you served in the French Direction du

Renseignement Militaire as a counterintelligence specialist. No wonder you're so good with your camera. As my Secretary of State, you will need to sharpen your paring knife. Foxxy, you will be the Secretary of the Interior. That department will be expanded to include most domestic issues. Rhoda, you are a master at juggling numerous projects and can do the work of three people. If you can keep Nick's ship afloat, quite frankly, you have to be a genius. You have your choice of U. N. Ambassador or Director of Homeland Security. Knowing you, you could probably do both jobs.

"The other important members of my cabinet, and my V.P., will also be female. I've not yet decided on my running mate, but I will ask your input on all appointments. We will have one or two token males so we're not accused of gender bias.

"Did the three of you read the books I recommended? Wow, that's a yes, yes, and a yes! We're off to a good start. Every person needs a mentor, a person who has blazed a trail for others to follow. For us, they appeared in the 1960s and '70s. This was the brave new world of feminism. Leaders like Betty Friedan, Gloria Steinem, Germaine Greer, and Irma Marie Wilde changed the course of history. For me, I. M. Wilde is the person who gave the most. She's been dead for fifteen years, but her fame is increasing because her contribution was so relevant.

"Wilde advanced the theory of feminist superiority by natural selection. She said that in almost all instances, a woman who was doing the job held previously by a man was far superior at that position. Since women had to endure terrible prejudice and numerous obstacles to achieve anything, when they finally did get a chance to perform, they outdid their male counterparts by a huge margin. As a result, women are now more capable than men. She said it is a natural evolutionary process.

"Wilde was the premier political feminist who defied Washington rules. She crashed the annual Alfalfa Club dinner, brought a bullhorn, and shouted down the then-president of the United States. You may or may not know about the Alfalfa Club. It's a social men-only club of politicians and businessmen which has included several presidents. Talk about infantile, the group was named for the alfalfa plant because of its supposed willingness to do anything for a drink. Can you hear them say yuk, yuk, yuk?

"In honor of the brave work of Irma Marie Wilde, we will call our new group the Wilde Party. Yes comrades, there will be three parties in the upcoming election: Republican, Democrat, and Wilde.

"By the time we're finished, my warrior mates, we will make the Amazons look like a bunch of flower-show mommies. Let's get busy, time for action. It's time for the Wilde Party."

# 55

"**H**ere I am once again in my Oval Office at three a.m., writing a diary entry. I gave my desk lamp with the green shade to Alfonso. He said something about a green alien video game and somehow that lamp fit the scene. In its place I have a custom, artisan-made mosaic glass lamp with a solid gold base. Shit, I can afford it. We are now worth $987 million, and we make 11 percent on our money. That is over $108 million a year in nice, safe interest. We have most of the money hidden. That is the full time job of my financial advisor. He does not work for anyone else, just the Hades family. I figure it this way. His annual retainer is 750K. Without this guy creating all these fabulous offshore accounts and tax shelters, we would be lucky to make 5 percent on our money. So we pay him $750K and he makes us $108 million. That works for me. The thing about making so much money, as my friends Adolph and Karl Krotch will tell you, is that it makes you want more. Do not let anybody tell you that less is more. More is more. I am going to leave charity to the liberal Democrats.

"Let me tell you something else, or more precisely, let me write my thoughts down for you. When there are two women whispering to each other in some corner, you can bet they are talking about another woman. When you see three women whispering to each other in that corner, you can bet they are talking about me. They think they are so smart, pretending not to like each other, pretending to have separate agendas, pretending to have my best interests at heart. I guarantee you they are plotting something. I must confess I have no proof of that, but I am a survivor. I did not get to this Oval Office by ignoring potential threats. It would be easy to put a stop to it right now and throw them all out. I could even do that to Nora, but she would get half the money. Plus her popularity is too high. She needs to stumble a bit, take a hit in the polls, and realize that she is in over her head. She is a woman who will instantly recognize the point where she stands to lose more than she will gain. At that point she will become as quiet as a church mouse, and again be a dutiful first lady.

"As for Foxxy and Rhoda, I think it's time for us to part company. I am replacing Rhoda as chief of staff with Helena Handbasket, the Chairpoison of the Republican National Committee. She will be soooo honored. She will be especially excited because she can stay on as Chairpoison of the RNC. I told her to hire my old journalism professor from college to be our next press secretary, replacing Foxxy Hart. The professor is rather simple and will do exactly as she is told. I cannot stand that bitch Handbasket, but having the RNC Chairpoison in plain sight will increase my power. Throwing the other two out will make it much harder for them to plot with Nora.

"I have brainstormed ways to keep Nora busy, but she is very reluctant to take my bait. She is about as maternal as a pole dancer, and hates being in the background. Come to think of it, what makes me think she would *want* to be vice president? After all, that is the number two.

"Just for a second there, I had the wild notion that she plans to challenge me for the Republican nomination. No, that is impossible. I have all the GOP senators and congressmen backing me, all my cabinet members, and the Chairpoison of the RNC is solidly in my corner. I have the Republican Krotch money. No, that notion is much too wild."

# 56

"Good morning, cabinet members. We have a lot on our agenda, and the most important item will be up first. You all know Bart Bassa, formerly of NSA, who is now director of Homeland Security. Bart has our backs, and has saved us all from embarrassment on many occasions. By removing email snooping duties from Sandcastle's sister, she can no longer wave the Freedom of Information Act in our faces to justify reading our private messages. But that solves the problem after the fact.

"Bart is terribly busy and short-staffed. He cannot possibly monitor all our communications, nor can he hold our hands during the dozens of press interviews we conduct on a daily basis. What he has suggested to me, and I completely agree with him, is to eliminate the need for electronic manipulation and deletion of emails.

"Bart is going to school us on the art of covering up. We all make gaffes. Some of us have big mouths. A couple of recent vice presidents come to mind."

"I hope you aren't talking about me, Mr. President."

"If the shoe fits, Percy, slip your foot into it. You might as well hire two staffers with brooms to sweep the trail clean behind you as you walk. You have yet to learn when a microphone is turned on and when it is turned off. You are not alone. It is how we all handle our gaffes that needs work. Bart, please take us on from here."

"Thank you, Mr. President. You make a great point about open microphones. Do you remember, during the 2000 presidential campaign, when George Bush and Dick Cheney thought their microphone was turned off? Bush called reporter Adam Clymer from *The New York Times* a 'major league asshole.' Cheney was heard to say the words 'big time.' Naturally the media went nuts, with *The New York Post* printing two pages about the comments. Here's where it went wrong. Mister Bush said, and this is a quote, 'I regret that a private comment I made to the vice-presidential candidate made it onto the public airwaves. I regret everybody heard what I said.'

"In my opinion, this was a huge mistake. Never admit to a wrongdoing! It's time to hone our skills in the sacred art of the political cover-up. The first rule to remember is always deny saying what you actually said. There are many ways to alter and disguise your comments. You need to camouflage your gaffe such that it *could* have been misinterpreted.

"For instance, if Bush had said, while expressing anger, 'What word did you just use? That's very vulgar and not something I want to hear again! Is that clear? I certainly did not use that word! What I said to the Vice President was, 'As sole reporter from the *Times* on this beat, Adam Clymer does a great job of covering all these campaign stops.' Dick Cheney agreed by saying what he always says when I make a good point. He says 'big time.' That's our code for, 'you nailed it, boss.' I say the same thing to him when he's on the money.'

"Reporters have a thing about accuracy. If you plant any doubt in their mind, they will freak out and pull the story. It's so important to remember the three 'nevers.' Never admit that you said what you said. Never apologize for what you said. Never give any media person the right to disagree with your explanation.

"And, here are three 'always' to remember. Always wait before explaining, to give you time to formulate your coverup. Always take offense at the reporter's impertinence and question his or her integrity and motivations for accusing you in the first place. Always utter a platitude about truth, justice, and the American way. That has worked for centuries.

"We must talk about how to camouflage your gaffe. Always remember, a lie told once might very well sound like a lie. But that same lie, told dozens of times by the entire Republican Party, will then become the truth. For instance, if you make a gaffe, the very first thing you do is talk about the intermittent microphone connection. The made-in-China microphones seem to cut in and out for no reason, you say. That is why it only picked up part of your statement, and everyone has taken it out of context. If every Republican complains about his or her microphone, it becomes the truth.

"Here's how to camouflage. Mr. Vice President, you were overheard to say, 'Those towelheads have got to learn that we mean business. I suggest we bomb them back to the Stone Age.' You have been ducking reporters' questions because you have been put on the defensive."

"I told you, Percy, you have a big mouth, and it has got to stop."

"Well, Mr. President, it is above my pay grade to comment on the vice president's actions. However, I will show him how to handle it. Let me present to you a similar situation from the Democratic archives. In March of 2004, then-presidential candidate John Kerry thought his microphone was off. He was quoted as saying 'Oh yeah, don't worry, man. We're going to keep pounding, let me tell you, we're just beginning to fight here. These guys are the most crooked, you know, lying group of people I've ever seen.'

"Now that is a long statement. He made a very weak explanation. What he should have said was that his microphone was broken and only picked up bits and pieces. His actual quote was, 'Oh yeah, don't worry man. We all want the same wonderful things for our country. My opponent and I are going to keep pounding until we prevail. Talk about our country's enemies? These guys are the most crooked, you know, lying group of people I've ever seen. Both Republicans and Democrats hate them.'

"Camouflage, gentlemen, camouflage! Mr. Vice President, here's what you say to the press about your towelhead comment. You complain about the bad microphone contacts. You then say that the comment everyone heard, 'Those towelheads have got to learn that we mean business. I suggest we bomb them back to the Stone Age,' is incorrect. What you actually said was 'Those hardworking people toil for hours in the sun and towel their heads to cool off. We owe it to them that we mean business. Our business is to improve their lot. I suggest that we can't let their enemies bomb them back to the Stone Age. They deserve to become productive members of the world community.'

"Remember to take offense, stand on your dignity, and utter platitudes about truth and the American way. Question the accuracy of the reporters' question. You will scare the shit out of them and force their news bureau to print a retraction."

# 57

# Eradicating Republican Rats

**It's vitally important to understand what the GOP rat is capable of. Do not underestimate your enemy.**

**GOP Tea Party Rat**

In many ways, GOP rats are truly remarkable. They can tread water for three days after being flushed down the toilet. They can tell 748 consecutive lies without disclosure or discovery. A GOP rat can fall as far as 50 feet and land uninjured. They can vote huge pay and benefit increases for themselves while actually lowering the minimum wage for the rest of us. A female rat can mate as many as 500 times during a six-hour period and can produce as many as 2,000 descendants in a year. And you think *you* enjoy sex! The

**GOP Moderate Rat**

average life expectancy for a brown rat is two to three years. For a GOP rat it's 90 to 95 years. Rats are very social, and closely mimic human psychology. They live almost invisibly among us and can be counted on to attack the food that we have in our pantries. You cannot ask them to stop this practice because a GOP rat has no conscience. In fact, the only two species that kill each other as a general policy during territorial disputes are GOP rats and man.

**GOP Bipartisan Rat (Extremely Rare)**

# What specific harm can a GOP rat do?

They carry disease. Millions of deaths were caused by the Bubonic Plague. They also cause leptospirosis, which damages the liver and kidneys; Lymphocytic choriomeningitis, transmitted through rat saliva and urine; and rat-bite fever. Think of *that* the next time you walk into a voting booth and are tempted to use that black felt-tipped pen to color in the Republican GOP rat-pack box. Never adopt a rat as a pet, no matter how cute you think they look, and no matter how eloquent their plea for votes. A rat is a rat is a rat. It can be nothing else.

**GOP Iowa Rats In Caucus**

What can be done to prevent GOP rats from entering your home, and what can be done to get rid of them once they have slipped past your defenses?

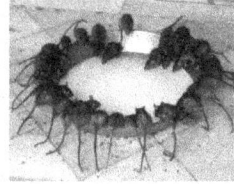

GOP Wisconsin Rats Discussing Dairy Subsidies

☐ We do not recommend humane removal treatments to get rid of rats. We strongly advise against catch and release programs. They don't deserve to be spared.

☐ The best defense is to make your home rat-proof. Plug up all holes bigger than 3/8" and keep your food and money out of sight.

☐ Adopt a Democratic cat from the animal shelter. Pin up photographs of Madoff, Limbaugh, McCarthy, Coulter, O'Reilly, and other GOP rats near her bed. This will make pussycat very angry and cause her to go on a killing rampage.

☐ Rely on your Yankee ingenuity and invent a better rat trap. GOP rats respond to ego, power, fame, and money traps. Once inside, they will never want to get out.

☐   If you suspect that you have a stubborn infestation in your dwelling, read aloud the writings of Thomas Paine, Henry David Thoreau, and Ralph Waldo Emerson. It will overload their neurons, causing instant death.

# For expert guidance on how to handle the intricacies of GOP rat removal, please contact:

Democratic National Headquarters, or your local animal shelter.

"Ow!  Helena, who put this trap under my desk?"

# 58

"**S**it down and shut up, young lady!  Alfonso, you had also better shut up and listen.  The two of you are dangerously close to huge, permanent trouble.  Is that clear?"

"What did we do now, Mom?  I thought my life, thus far, has been smooth and without unfriendly incidents."

"Petunia, I said shut up.  Bart Bassa has become a friend of the family, and from him I learned that...."

"Why do I get the feeling that he isn't going to turn out to be my friend?"

"Alfonso, one more interruption and you are finished.

"Bart Bassa monitors all domestic communications for Homeland Security.  He has sent me copies of your tweets and text messages for the last month.  We are going to review them now.  Bart has taught your father and me a great deal about tweets, twiddles, twerps, twerks, and twaddles, or whatever the hell else you're calling them.  It's no wonder you kids no longer know how to speak English."

"I didn't know we had a Big Brother watching over us."

"According to Bart, there are 500 million Twitter users, and 40 percent of all tweets are pointless babble.  350 billion text messages are sent every month. At least you're making work for the NSA, and the phone companies rich. At ten cents a tweet, coming and going, that's a lot of birdseed. Pretty soon, Alfonso, you will stare at me with one of your fake dumb looks and ask, 'What's a pen?' Your children won't even be able to write their own damned names. No one will remember how to speak, and spoken language will disappear. All you will be able to do is press buttons on a keypad. You sure will have evolved some talented thumbs. Darwin would be proud.

"Just before I told the two of you to sit down, you were texting. Were you texting each other?"

"Sometimes we text each other."

"For Christ's sake, you're sitting seven feet apart, why the hell don't you just have a conversation?"

"What's a *conversation*?"

"Okay Alfonso, I warned you. Give me your God-damned pod or pad, or whatever the hell you call it! You too, Petunia, hand it over! Now let's see what was so important.

"What's this Petunia? 'RT, TBH, DA MISTWEET WAS OH AND NOT K. HE SAID SAFRA, BUT IT WAS A DWEET. HE'S A SF.' Who did you send this to, and what does it mean?"

"I sent it to all the people on my Twitter account."

"How many people do you have on your Twitter account?"

"I have 17, 578,232 as of this morning."

"17 million!"

"That's not such a big deal,  Katy Perry has 63,810,164, Justin Bieber has 59,563,491, Barack Obama has 53,604,487, and Taylor Swift has 51,132,675.  Dad has 72,584,219, so my followers are small by comparison.  You should get an account, since you're so ambitious."

"That son of....so that's how he's climbing in the polls.  What does your text message mean?"

"It's not a text message, it's a tweet.  Text messages are aimed at a much smaller audience. Let me see it again, I didn't memorize it.  I was commenting on a tweet my language arts teacher posted yesterday to his Twitter account.  Actually I was resending my message.  Okay, (RT) means Retweet, (TBH) to be honest, (MISTWEET) the mistweet that he regrets sending (WAS OH) was overheard (AND NOT K) and not cool.  (HE SAID SAFRA) He said suck a fat rat's ass (BUT IT WAS A DWEET), but it was a drunken tweet.  (HE'S A SF) He's a sick fuck."

"Petunia, this is what you are sending to 17, 578,232 people?"

"That is correct.  You should see all the responses I got.  He's in big trouble and will probably lose his job.  Do you want a man like that teaching your daughter?"

"I don't guess so, but couldn't you have been more diplomatic?"

"What is *diplomatic*?  Do you want me to open an account for you?"

"Great idea, when do we start?  Can I post photographs?"

# 59

"It has been almost seven months since my last late-night journal entry. Actually, I have been so busy that I have not written *any* journal entries since that last one. I am a total creature of habit, so naturally it is three a.m., and I am sitting in the Oval Office. Do you know what really chaps me? That someone else, possibly even of a different party like Damnocrat Bernice Sandcastle, could one day be sitting in this very chair. It does not seem right, somehow. I went to all the trouble of lying, conniving, wheeling, dealing, threatening, cajoling, intimidating, manipulating, ignoring, shouting, pontificating, stealing, and glad-handing, and I do not get to keep this mansion, or even this one fucking office chair. Life is just not fair.

"A lot has happened in the last seven months. I have a new chief of staff. Helena Handbasket is now my vice president. I promoted her because she is a very important and persuasive woman. She will be an asset in the next election. She is abrasive and will debate well. No doubt about it, she is tearing it up as vice president and will make a wonderful running mate. I must confess that we did diddle a time or two. I cannot work closely with a female without attempting a few diddles. We did not hit it off, however. It was like having sex with a dead mackerel. She just lay there like rigor mortis had set in. I have learned that women who wear navy blue business suits and who carry leather attaché cases are preoccupied with audits, paper trails, accounting, quantification, and quorums. They never seem to carry the right size condoms. But she looks good next to me on the campaign buttons. She has perfected the art of the Republican smile. When a Republican smiles, when you see that toothy grin, you never know what is inside their heads. I read an article in the *Republican Journal* on how to smile for the camera. They have some good advice. All you have to do is envision your hand being in someone else's pocket. That usually brings instant joy. The smile will appear genuine.

"I will not even discuss what happened to Percy. He is an idiot.

"I had my doubts about Nora wanting to be vice president. I was right. As most of you already know, she is hot on the trail of the presidency. Looks like we have a three-way race. When she first announced her intention, I threw a major fit and we separated for a month. I would not stop cursing and screaming, so she made me move into the Lincoln Room after I threw Foxxy out. She said the only way she would take me back is if I hired men for my press secretary and my chief of staff. So, that is what I did. I missed our fights. So did the children. The calm was driving both of them crazy, so we reconciled.

"A funny thing happened. As you probably know, Foxxy Hart, Madeleine Soufflé, and Rhoda Dendron are on her team. Since she doesn't have any men in her inner circle, and since I do not have any women in mine, we have been behaving like the first gerbils. It is kind of kinky. The more we try to tear each other apart politically, the more we screw. Go figure. She keeps on needling me. She has been telling everyone that someday soon I will be the first gentleman, except that I am really no gentleman.

"I am looking forward to the debates. It will be very interesting, because the three of us have nothing in common, politically that is. Sandcastle will probably pick some Greenie, mushroom collecting, tree-hugger as her running mate. Nora will probably pick some Amazon with a poison-tipped spear. I have got the best running mate, the best political machine, and the most money. I have caught up to Nora in the polls with my skillful use of Twitter, and the three of us are in a virtual tie. I have asked the Krotch brothers to doctor the figures, so perhaps we can falsify the data to show that we are ahead. Americans love a winner. That is why there are so few Houston Astros fans."

# 60

"**G**ood morning, Euwee. Before we get down to work, my daughter and her class are making a quick visit to the Oval Office as part of their field trip. This is her political science class, and they are due at any moment. Ah, here they are now.

"Hello, Petunia, and welcome to you all. This is Euwee Crinkle, my new chief of staff. You must be Frau Hymnler. Petunia often speaks favorably of your school. I hope my daughter is not too stubborn, obstinate, and wrongly opinionated to distract the other students. If she is, I assure you she that takes after her mother."

"Das is goot, Mr. President. Vee love Petunia. Vee also love Nora. Either of you vood make oon splendid president."

"Dad, did you ever stop to think that you and Mom running against each other guarantees that Bernice Sandcastle will win? You are both so good at sniping at each other, you are doing Sandcastle's work for her. Shouldn't you get her out of the way before you cut each other's throats?"

"Then tell your mother to drop out, put on her fuzzy slippers, and be a dutiful and supportive first lady. Petunia, this is not the time nor the place to discuss her candidacy. Do you want any information for your class? We have some beautiful brochures about how we redecorated the Lincoln Room, and here is another about all the different kinds of roses in the Rose Garden. Oh yes, and here is one that I wrote about the physical requirements for becoming a female congressional intern."

"Mr. President, vee vere vondering von ting. Alice would like to ask you a question."

"Yes, Frau Hymnler, I will be happy to answer Alice's question."

"Thank you, Mr. President. It's so awesome to be here, and I just love Nora. My question is about currency. You had Benjamin Franklin's portrait removed from the hundred-dollar bill and your own put on it. How come there are no women like I. M. Wilde on any of our bills?"

"Christ, Nora has warped Petunia, and Petunia has warped the entire class. As far as I am concerned, Alice, Irma Marie Wilde is one of the top members of the Amazon Lunatic Fringe. Class, you have not done your homework. We have a woman gracing one piece of our currency, and it is not Lady Liberty. Susan B. Anthony is on the dollar. Are you aware of that, Alice, Petunia?"

"Big deal, that's not a bill, that's a coin. They don't mint them any more. Do you know why, because the damn thing is just slightly bigger than a quarter. At least they could have made it the same size as the Eisenhower dollar, but no, it was a puny coin that confused everyone. They were discontinued just after they were put into circulation."

"Maybe you should go find some. They are probably worth more for their collector's value than George Washington is. If you want to see I. M. Wilde's portrait on any of our bills, someone else will have to be removed, unless, of course you want to propose a new denomination like a three-dollar bill, or how about a nine-dollar-

and-ninety-nine cents bill?  They can use them in New York City. That is something a Democrat would propose.  Why not talk to the Treasurer of the United States, Rosa Gumataotao Rios, and present your idea to her?  You are so worked up that no woman is on our paper money, but did you ever stop to think that every single treasurer since 1949 has been a woman?  Ms. Rios is the sixth Latina to be treasurer."

"Am I supposed to be excited about that?  Dad, you know the structure of any corporation.  Who has the most power?"

"Okay, Petunia, I will play your game and answer the question. Depending on the company's structure, the most power is held by the CEO, president, or chairman of the board."

"Exactly.  So does a company president have more power than his secretary?  The answer is, of course he does.  But not in our government.  Rosa Rios is the treasurer, but the Secretary of the Treasury has all the power.  The present secretary is Coin Goldman.  He's the one who makes all the financial decisions. Rosa Rios just has her token signature on our paper money. Alexander Hamilton was the first secretary, and he served in 1789. There has *never* been a female Secretary of the Treasury in our history.  Why is that?"

"Petunia, that is because Congress could never find a qualified woman to lead the Treasury.  That is also why there has not been a female president of the United States.  Some day that may change, but it will have to be long after I am gone.  What is the foremost American symbol, and what does *he* hold in his hand?  It is a bald eagle, and he holds thirteen sharp-pointed, phallic, male arrowheads."

"Well, bald is right, but he or she also holds an olive branch."

"Yes, I know.  That disturbs me as well. I am trying to get the eagle replaced with a Komodo Dragon."

# 61

"**W**hew, Euwee! Those kids are a handful. You have children, do you not?"

"Yes, Mr. President, we have three. My wife Clara tells them what to think, and they mostly ignore what I say."

"Aha, we *are* turning into a matriarchy. You know, I have an idea. Before we get into today's business, we should entertain the possibility of a currency change. You can bet that the first lady put those ideas into Petunia's head. I will bet that she is preparing to introduce some cockamamie legislation in her platform to put I. M. Wilde's portrait on our money."

"Yes, Mr. President. But don't forget, sir, you have a tattoo touchup at two p.m."

"Thanks for reminding me. I will not break *that* appointment. Move the others out if you need to. So, let us look at who we can remove from our money for Wilde. Maybe we could put her portrait on food stamps. No, that may have the opposite effect, and she could become champion of the downtrodden. Let us see. Here is what we have. I keep every denomination in my money clip for good luck:

On the 1-dollar bill is George Washington
2 Thomas Jefferson

5 Abraham Lincoln. Now there's a possibility. Abe was a Republican back when Republicans were more like Democrats. His Emasculation Procrastination does not impress me at all. I am not into minorities.

10 Alexander Hamilton

20 Andrew Jackson

50 Ulysses S. Grant

100 Nick Hades. Ben Franklin was on the 100, but he was not even a president. That is why I replaced him.

500 William McKinley

1000 Grover Cleveland

5000 James Madison

10,000 Salmon P. Chase  Whoa! Do you not love the fact that the biggest bill of all does not have a president on it?  It has a banker. That is the American way.

"You know, Euwee, the current minimum wage is $7.25, or $15,080 per year.  In my opinion that is plenty good enough.  The Walmann family, which owns WalWart, has assets of 157.4 billion dollars.  If you divide the minimum-wage earner's salary of $15,080 into the Walmann's $157 billion, you get 10,418,047 sheeple who are earning minimum wage.  Therefore, one family has as much money as 10,418,047 Americans.

"So, who are we going to listen to, some 60-year-old greeter at WalWart who has no medical benefits, or the powerful and influential family that employs her?

"I know what we will do.  Let us remove the portrait of Abraham Lincoln from the copper penny and replace him with Irma Marie Wilde.  Pennies are a pain in the ass.  We will beat Nora to the punch.  Let us get a press release ready.  This kind of segues into what I wanted to discuss in the first place.  Lincoln was a

Federalist, and I am a States Rights kind of guy, unless state interests are in conflict with my interests....erm....*federal* interests.

"Speaking of pennies, Governor Tuppence of Indiana needs our help. There is big trouble in my home state. What was originally a wonderful social experiment has turned into a left-wing debacle. The poor man and his brave Republican legislature tried to introduce a religious freedom bill. And what has happened to him as a result? He is being crucified.

"This is the summary paper that thirty law professors had the gall to write, contradicting Governor Tuppence's claim that his bill would guarantee religious freedom."

*In our expert opinion, the clear evidence suggests otherwise and unmistakably demonstrates that the broad language of the proposed state RFRA will more likely create confusion, conflict, and a wave of litigation that will threaten the clarity of religious liberty rights in Indiana while undermining the state's ability to enforce other compelling interests....Members of the public will then be asked to bear the cost of their employer's, their landlord's, their local shopkeeper's or a police officer's private religious beliefs.*

"What a crock! Every time we try to take a giant step backward, there is a group of free-thinkers who are trying to pull us in the other direction. It is no wonder I cannot accomplish anything....I mean, hell, you know what I mean.

"Memories Pizza in Walkerton, Indiana, population 2248, had the courage to put up a large sign proudly affirming their religious beliefs. Are they not allowed to decide whom they invite into their own home and restaurant for dinner?

"Their sign said that they did not want to serve those who are:

Gay fruits
Lesbian fruits
Transgendered fruits
Transsexual fruits
Bisexual fruits
Asexual fruits
Unwed mothers
Food stamp leeches
Welfare recipients
Atheists
Jews
Buddhists
Muslims
Drug users
Liberals
Socialists
Humanitarians
and Italians

Since there are only 2248 citizens in Walkerton, that left four who made the cut. They are the family of App L. Pye, president of the Indiana National Bank. Memories made them a very big, and a very delicious pizza, one which will be remembered, like their sign, for all the ages.

"I want you to send an email to Governor Tuppence and offer him assistance. We can provide nerve gas, Abrams tanks, Special Forces units, portable interrogation centers, and brainwashing chaplains to re-indoctrinate non-believers who refuse to conform to normal religious beliefs and/or normal sexuality."

# 62

"This planning and strategy session of the I. M. Wilde Party is called to order. Rhoda, pass me those olives. Foxxy, did you get the information on Club La Vela?"

"I did, Nora, but what do we want with La Vela?"

"See if you can guess. Live up to your name, Foxxy. What is La Vela?"

"It's a nightclub in Panama City Beach, Florida."

"Right, what kind of nightclub?"

"It's the largest nightclub in America. Wait a minute. Is that where we're going to have our party convention?"

"Bingo! Foxxy, you nailed it. We can't afford to rent Yankee friggin' Stadium, or Kansas, like our opponents can, and we don't need to. Here's why. La Vela holds 6,000 patrons and they have many different dance rooms. They have dedicated rooms for house music, hip hop, rock, and one that features foam blowers.

"I know what Americans want. It makes no difference whether it's watching the Super Bowl, *Saturday Night Live*, or a political convention. They want to be entertained. What would you rather see, a stoned-out western movie actor talking to an empty chair, or your favorite singer pulsing on stage surrounded by strobe lights?

All those corn-fed old women in their red, white, and blue straw hats are so yesterday.

"After every political speech we will have another act. It's all about ratings, ladies, ratings. After I pick my vice president, we will have Snotty Droopy Dingo Doggy play his most thumping music while he bumps and grinds on stage.

"Don't forget, we will get press coverage on every network. We will not have to pay for this. Foxxy, your job is to make sure we are live-streamed into all the major computer servers. Which is more effective, a dry convention with talking heads that is only partially broadcast on one or two television networks, or our Wilde Party convention streamed into every computer in America and beyond? Which convention will get the highest ratings, and which candidate will America vote for? Madeleine, you have a question."

"I love the Club La Vela idea, Nora, but shouldn't we concentrate on a platform and our talking points? Rhoda and I were wondering if you feel comfortable attacking Nick."

"You do make a great general, Madeleine. That is exactly why we are meeting today, to form an attack strategy. Don't worry about me. I have absolutely no hesitation in going after Nick. As far as I'm concerned, all is fair in love, war, and presidential campaigns. So, any ideas on what we can do? Yes, Rhoda, what you got, woman?"

"The first thing we need to mention is that Nick is getting fat. He is sending the wrong message to America. If the president isn't health conscious, neither will Americans be."

"Excellent! We need photos of his stretched-out Komodo Dragon tattoo. Madeleine, can you get those?"

"If you can get him naked, I will get the photos. How about the idea of unprotected sex? Nick doesn't believe in safe measures. How can we exploit that?"

"We can have a half-dozen pregnant unwed mothers in a room talking about how their boyfriends abandoned them. We can then superimpose Nick on screen with the words, "Who will accept responsibility for his actions if the president won't?"

"Excellent, Rhoda! Any other ideas?"

"He has a preoccupation with congressional interns and wrote a brochure with specific female physical requirements for hiring. We should exploit that."

"I don't know, Rhoda. I was thinking of writing one myself about male interns. We don't want to appear hypocritical."

"He keeps appointing new vice presidents. We should imply that they quit because he is impossible to work with. He isn't a team player but does what is best for himself at the expense of the country. How's this: 'America doesn't need a selfish president, we need a man of the people.'"

"That's a bit cliché. How about, 'When you need a big brother or a friend to walk alongside you in times of trouble, the president is sitting at home playing violent video games,' something like that."

"Not perfect, but much better. Please pass the olives."

# 63

"**J**en, we have already made history. Everybody in the Democratic Party said that I had zero chance of getting its nomination for president. I ran against two mainstream candidates and won. I didn't win by much, but the bottom line is the bottom line. So here we are in a three-way race. The polls have Nick Hades slightly ahead, due to all his orange terrorist alerts and fear-mongering. He already has a running mate in Helena Handbasket. She's a sharp-tongued bitch who loves money, fame, and power as much as he does. They make a great team.

"We have the psychological advantage, however, because Handbasket has had too much exposure. The American people love the flavor of the week, but they soon tire of whatever celebrity is hot at the moment. Her popularity, when computed apart from Nick's, has actually dropped two points in the last month. She may not be the sterling asset the president bargained for. We, on the other hand, can choose a fresh face with some pizzazz. Jen, this election is not going to be politics as usual. It will take more than money to buy the presidency. It will take media savvy, and honesty. If the American people can't tell the difference between opportunistic hucksters and someone who is honestly wanting to serve the people, I won't stand a chance. I'm hoping they can. I'm counting on it, or I wouldn't be running."

"Bernice, we're in third place, slightly behind Nora Hades. She may be a bigger threat than her husband."

255

"I don't think so, Jen. Nora is all flash. She knows nothing about the issues. We'll see where she is after the debates. The American people love to watch her, and find her very amusing. In the end, they must decide who will help them get their children through college, who will get them the jobs they deserve, who will restore their country's pride and world stature. I question my own ability to perform these Herculean tasks, but at least the Democratic Party platform has incorporated most of my ideas. I can't remember when there was such a definitive choice between candidates. Nick and I are oil and water. He's the oil, of course. We are promise and pompous, we are an eagle and a dodo bird, we are reason and treason, we are a Democrat and a Republican, enough said. Americans always vote for whoever has the most TV exposure during sports events. That's what worries me. My campaign staff is readying similar ads, but they just don't sound right coming from me.

"I'm too much like Eleanor Roosevelt or Sonia Sotomayor. I'm introspective, and a quiet thinker. I don't wear a tight white sweater or red sequined knickers. I don't have teased blonde hair, and I don't chew gum with my mouth open. Naturally I won't play well in Texas.

"The Libertarian wing of the Republican Party has merged with the Tea Party wing. They call themselves *Libertea*. Nick Hades has embraced their ideas and is stumping around the country with what looks like the same Revolutionary force that defended Bunker Hill. Taking that into consideration, I have prepared the next email message for our website, and the MoveOver.orgy website."

**Nick Hades knows exactly where he is going. Here is what he is going to do for America if reelected.**

- He will put two black-powder muskets in every umbrella stand, and a tri-cornered hat in every closet.
- Indoor plumbing could be a real possibility for your home.
- Hitching posts will be constructed in front of every U.S. Post Office.
- He will permit additional tariffs on tea.
- He will continue his friendship with King George III.
- He will find a more efficient way to harvest cotton.
- He will permit women to show their ankles in public.
- Women will be allowed to go to market unaccompanied by their husbands.
- People of color will eventually have the same rights as women.
- He will build a fifteen-foot fence, topped with barbed wire, around the entire perimeter of our thirteen colonies.

Vote for Nick Hades. He will return us to 1770, when America was part of England.

This message was brought to you by Bernice Sandcastle, who approves of its content.

# 64

"It is about time we left Washington behind for a little R and R in the Montana wilderness. Well, it is *sort* of wilderness when you leave the lodge. Jboo, Itch, let us not talk about the upcoming election, my daffy wife Nora, and especially not Bitch Sandcastle. We are here to unwind, and to take advantage of what America has to offer.

"Let us look at the game identification cards the Republican National Committee prepared for our hunt. And do not forget, the day after tomorrow we will take our fishing rods to the Yellowstone River and try to snag those elusive Montana sardines. I hear they put up a whale of a fight when hungry. It seems they are *always* hungry, at least according to these game cards. Itch, why do you not hold up the first card. Do not look at the back, and we will see if we can identify it."

"I believe that is a big-horny sheep."

"I don't think so, Itch. I think it is a medium-horny antelope."

"Nope, it says it's a sheepfawn. There's a caution about getting too near them. All shots should be taken from no closer than 400 yards."

"Jboo, what kind of guns did you bring?"

"Well, Mr. President, since these Montana sheepfawns can be mighty fierce, I brought my .458 Winchester magnum with steel-tipped hollow points. In case one gets too close, I have a Smith and Wesson .500 magnum revolver loaded with incendiary explosive bone-crusher shells."

"Good idea, Jboo, you do not want to be gored by a sheepfawn. Hold up the next card."

"Mr. President, I think the RNC is trying to fool us. That isn't game, that's a cow."

"Jboo, you may be correct. Itch, what does it say on the back of the card?"

"It's game all right, Mr. President. According to the description, it's a black and white spotted Jersey deer. They are supposed to be very tasty, especially the ones with all those udders."

"Hold up the next card. What the hell is that? It looks positively prehistoric. Please read the description."

"It says it's a web-footed, Wall Street crockogator. It's the meanest animal in America."

"What's a web-footed, Wall Street crockogator?"

"It's an animal with a head at both ends. All it does is eat everything in sight, and it can't shit. They advise staying away from them unless you have a black and white spotted Jersey deer to offer as a sacrifice."

"Yuk, look at this guy. What is he?"

"It looks like a huge rat with lots of fur and long, curly tusks. My guess is a long-tailed wolf. What do you think, Jboo?"

"Oops, they made a mistake including this one. That's Trott Jogger. He's the Republican Tea Party Governor of Wisconsin. He's staying at the next lodge."

"Do you know what I think, fellow sportsmen? I think hunting these creatures may be a bit risky without military backup. Did we alert the Montana National Guard to be on standby?"

"No, Mr. President, we did not."

"Perhaps we should stick to fishing instead of hunting. Tomorrow morning, nice and early, when the dew is evaporating from the prairie grass and the golden sun is barely up in Big Sky country, we will sneak quietly to the banks of the Yellowstone River and catch Montana sardines."

"Mr. President?"

"What is it, Itch? You look hesitant."

"Perhaps we should shoot them instead. Better to be safe, don't you think?"

"Excellent idea! We will leave our fishing rods at the lodge and bring our fragmentation grenades."

# 65

"**I**tch, Jboo, sit down and have some artichoke hearts. This time I did something different. Now that the traitor Madeleine Soufflé works for Nora, we have a new cook. I hand-picked her, and she is one hot tamale. Nora thought she was so slick restricting me to a male chief of staff and press secretary, but she forgot about the family cook. So I hired Fifi, and yes, that is her real name, so do not laugh. And her last name is LaFlamme. That is also her real last name, so do not laugh about that, either. Fifi created a jalopeno pepper and hot horseradish marinade for my artichoke hearts. I spoon them on top of the peanut butter and jelly sandwiches and wash it down with spiked apple cider. You would not believe the energy that food gives me! I can positively sprint from here to the water fountain and on to the men's room. You want some? Okay, maybe later.

"We had a great time in Montana. Pitching fragmentation grenades into the Yellowstone River was a hoot. We got lots of fish, but unfortunately they were not whole. All we wound up with was fish puree, but it sure was tasty. We did get a scare when that sardine jumped out of the river onto the bank and snapped at you, Jboo. Did you see those teeth? Good thing we had Navy Seal backup. They arrived at the last minute, and I was sure glad to see them. We got some great political mileage out of our fishing trip. The photographers got us at our best. That was a great photo op close to the election. The Kevlar helmets and flak vests were a nice touch. I do enjoy opportunities to display my leadership.

263

"Speaking of leadership, we need to make some adjustments to our government agencies. As true and loyal Republicans, the three of us have learned to bait and switch our way to power. We have to convince the American sheeple we are planning to support those agencies we choose to dissolve. They have never learned to decipher the code of Republican doublespeak."

"How do we do that, Mr. President? I get the feeling the master has been at work. I also get the feeling that there will be more green in our pockets."

"Right you are, Itch. You have not spent your tenure as Senate majority leader with your eyes closed. This is what I plan to do. Let us start with the Environmental Protection Agency. We know that *way* too much money is appropriated annually for these glorified tree-huggers. This is money that can be used for F-35s, and as you say, Itch, green for our wallets.

"This is what we do. We create a big fanfare about a brave new EPA initiative. We want the EPA to monitor air and water pollution around every single U.S. military base. In the past they have been strictly off limits. We divert EPA money directly to the bases for the 'cleanup.' We siphon some of that off the top for administrative expenses. That is us, of course. In the end, the EPA is reduced in size by three-fourths, the money is redistributed to our beloved military, and a contract for 200 more F-35s goes to Lockness Marin.

"Second example. I am sure the three of us agree that the Food and Drug Administration is a royal pain. First of all, our predecessors, in their infinite stupidity, combined the separate and distinctly different worlds of drugs and food. That is like combining apples and pears. It does not wash. So I will write an executive order to separate the FDA into two groups, the Food Administration and the Drug Administration. I will claim to do this in order to strengthen both groups. They are too *important* to be lumped together into one agency. Since they will be half their former size, they will expect their budgets to be cut by 50 percent. However, I will trim each budget by 75 percent. The extra funds will go into building more F-35s, and we happily pocket some more administrative expenses.

"Third example. Federal funding for PBS. Now that is the kind of spirit I expect from both of you. I heard your highly audible groans. They have been a real problem, especially since the Krotch brothers give them hard cash. In this case I am going to *increase* their budget by 50 percent. At the same time, I am instituting an executive order for equal programming. I will make it illegal for any news organization to produce shows that are derogatory and critical of the president, that would be me, without giving equal time to the GMG. What is the GMG? It is my new agency, the Government Media Group. They will be producing shows that present us in the best possible light. We already had a crew with us in Montana filming our fishing expedition. Half of all PBS airtime will now be controlled by the GMG.

"Excuse me, got to run to the loo."

# 66

# Do Away With Republican Slugs

**What hasn't been said and written about the repulsiveness of God's slimiest creatures? Is it possible to coexist with GOP slugs? We give you the vital information needed for survival.**

GOP Slugs About To Mate

GOP Female Slug After Spa Treatments

Here are the main sub-groups of slugs:

Orthurethra – These slugs live in the U.S. Capitol.

Pupilloidea – These slugs congregate in the U.S. Capitol.

Gastrodontoidea – These slugs can thrive in the U.S. Capitol.

Helixarionoidea – These slugs have taken up residence in the U.S. Capitol.

Knowledge is power.  No matter what kind of slug you are looking for, he/she can be found in Slime Central, the U. S. Capitol.

Slugs have two kinds of tentacles on their heads. The upper set is light sensing, and the lower set has the sense of smell.

Slugs are hermaphrodites:  they have both male and female reproductive organs.  They truly can go fuck themselves.  This is something we have been telling them for a very long time.  For Republican slugs it *is* anatomically possible!

A slug secretes two types of mucus as it moves.  A thin mucus spreads from the foot's center to its edges, and a thick mucus spreads from front to back.  They also produce thick mucus that coats the whole body of the slug.  You can always tell where a GOP slug has been by the mucus trail.  Other slugs coming across a slime trail find it useful in locating a mate of the same species.

Slugs practice *apophallation*.  Their penises curl like corkscrews, and during mating they

**GOP Slugs In Easter Clothes**

**GOP Slugs At RNC Orgy**

become entangled in their mate's genitalia. Apophallation allows them to separate themselves by one or both of the slugs chewing off the other's penis. They are still able to mate, using only the female parts of their reproductive systems. Now is this the kind of creature you want in Congress?

GOP slugs feed on tomatoes, strawberries, flowers of all kinds, sub-prime carrots, peas, apples, speculation cabbage, begonias, energy stocks, hollyhocks, and narcissus. (But not on narcissists, out of professional courtesy.)

**GOP Slug President Addressing His Faithful At The RNC Slime Convention**

# Strategies for long-term slime control and GOP slug eradication.

# You will need vigorous resolve, super-strong determination, lots of beer, and a strong stomach.

- ☐ Vigilantism is highly recommended. It is best to slug-hunt at night. Use a flashlight and disposable gloves. Skewer the GOP slugs with a stick and drop them into a bucket of water.
- ☐ Follow any slime trails that you notice. Look carefully around your cesspool or leach field.
- ☐ Slugs hate garlic, mint, chives, and reason.
- ☐ Place donkey droppings around your garden.
- ☐ Pour beer liberally on the rotten slimeballs. Enjoy watching them dissolve into a puddle of gelatinous goo.

# For professional help, contact:

Al Franken – Democratic Senator, Minnesota

"Euwee, do you want a beer?"

# 67

"**T**omorrow is the big day, Dr. Gung.  It's the day I will be debating my husband and Bernice Sandcastle.  We will be on live TV.  Isn't it exciting?"

"How do you feel about that, Mr. President?"

"I think Nora is an idiot.  She will do anything so people can watch her on TV.  I am sure she will wear a see-through skirt so everyone can see her red-sequined knickers.  We agreed to reconcile our differences as long as we do not talk about her candidacy, so why the hell are you bringing it up?"

"I think the two of you can serve as role models for couples everywhere.  I'm proud that you haven't shot or stabbed each other yet.  How do you kids feel about this unusual situation?"

"I support Mom, and I support the I. M. Wilde party.  Men have ruined the world.  Look at Alfonstupido.  He agrees with Dad, and all he does is play violent video games."

"Petunia, if having a big mouth made you a leader, you and your Wilde women would be queens of all the Earth.  You don't know anything about the future.  I know what warfare will be like.  We will have drones with Gatling guns and 500-pound bombs.  We will have driverless tanks and remote-controlled mobile artillery pieces.  We will have pilotless Cobra attack helicopters.   Entire  battles  will  be  fought  by  one  person watching a giant screen. I intend to someday be in charge of our military. I am going to be the top general. My joystick will control thousands of pieces of unmanned military equipment. My Russian counterpart will be doing the same thing. I intend to be better than he is. The very survival of America will depend on my skills, so back off, Pizza-Face. Dr. Gung would say that you have penis envy. No matter how Wilde you act, you will never be as Wilde as me. Isn't that right, Doctor?"

"I see you and Petunia have made progress. At least you're talking to each other. I don't see the death stars and brass knuckles that you brought to our last session."

"I do have my Malaysian throwing knife stuck in my belt in case she messes with my game console."

"I wouldn't stoop to touch your damned console, and I'm not afraid of your useless throwing knife. Ha, ha, I dulled the point on the bench grinder in the boiler room."

"Mom, Pizza-Face ruined my throwing knife!"

"Alfonso, Petunia, have you ever thought of helping each other instead of all this constant rancor?"

"Mom, I will gladly help Alfonso. I will help him fall off the White House roof."

"Mr. President, what are you and Nora going to do after tomorrow night's debate? Does the family plan on eating out?"

"Oh yes, Dr. Gung, we will be eating out, or taking in food every night. Our new chef wasn't hired for her skill at *baking* buns. Nick, you must think I'm fast asleep. I hired a male chef to replace your Fifi. As soon as she leaves, we will have dinner together again. He intends to replace your artichoke hearts with Brussels sprouts."

"We will see about that, you stupid bitch! I will teach you to mess with my artichoke hearts! This is war!"

"Nick! Nora! Stop it! Stop fighting! Put that paperweight down! Stop it!"

# 68

"**G**ood evening, ladies and gentlemen. I'm Jim Trapezoid from FLOX News. Welcome to the first of what promises to be three very lively presidential debates. These debates are sponsored by the CPD, the Commission on Presidential Debates, and is headed by the former chairs of the Democratic and Republican National Committees."

"See, right there we have a problem. The I. M. Wilde Party had no part in planning and preparing tonight's debate. A third party is at an automatic disadvantage before we even begin."

"Mrs. Hades, we will attempt...."

"It's Ms. Hades, and I don't care what you attempt. Why is my podium three inches shorter than the other two? The people at home may not recognize that it is, but it will register with them subconsciously. I'm standing on this five-inch wooden block to compensate for this deliberate attempt to diminish my candidacy. And why is the president in the middle? He is automatically the center of attention. I'm all the way on the left, and, as we know, the eye moves from left to right, so Bernice's position is also better. I demand extra time to compensate for these deliberate slights."

"Ms. Hades, you can refer to that in the debate. I'm sorry to have to cut you off here, but if I don't, I will have to give the other two candidates equal time."

"The only way you can cut her off is by putting her in a muzzle."

"That is a symbolic silencing of the female, and is something the American people should expect from Nick Hades. I agree with Nora on this one."

"Thank you, Bernice. Please continue, Mr. Trapezoid."

"With me here tonight are the esteemed co-anchors of FLOX News, Hymie Wart and Bill O'Hara. Here are the rules for tonight's debate, as agreed upon by both major candidates."

"Up yours, Trapezoid."

"A coin toss determines who gets to answer the first question, the remaining major party candidate will go second, and the third party candidate will, fittingly, go third. There will be no opening statements, but each candidate will have three minutes for a closing statement. In our first segment, Hymie and Bill will alternate questioning. In the second segment, we will take questions from members of the audience. Each candidate will have two minutes to answer. The opposing candidates will each have one minute to respond in rebuttal. At the moderator's discretion, I will extend discussion time by thirty seconds if I feel it is warranted."

"Jim, you had better plan on giving Nora and Bernice another four minutes each after that, because there is not a man on this Earth who can keep either of them from screeching for at least five minutes. I wish you luck, pal."

"Thank you, Mr. President. I anticipated that eventuality, so I brought this huge fire bell. If either of the women goes over the allotted time, I will pound it. It's so loud that, believe me, all conversation will stop because no one will be able to hear anything above the awful clanging. I will toss the coin to see who goes first. If it's heads, the president speaks first. If it's tails, Senator Sandcastle goes second. It's tails. Nick Hades won the coin toss and will answer the first question, which is from Hymie."

"Thank you, Jim. Good evening, candidates, and good evening, ladies and gentlemen. Mr. President, some people are upset that even though your family is worth close to one billion dollars, you pay only 2 percent income tax. Why is that, sir?"

"Great question, Hymie. Nora supervises all our tax shelters. She's the financial genius of the family, so you will have to ask her."

"Your response, Ms. Hades."

"I'm surprised at your question, Mr. Wart. As you know, every candidate must file full financial disclosure forms. It's a well known and celebrated Republican fact that no rich people pay any taxes. Taxes are something poor and middle class people pay. That is why I am now running on the Wilde Party ticket. We are going to reverse that trend and bring back true graduated income tax. The IRS is now the enemy of the American people. When I am president, the IRS will become your friend, and all the fat cats will be a lot skinnier.

"Your response, Senator Sandcastle."

"My response is shock and amazement. Nora Hades is Queen of Denial. She has been living in super-luxury for all these years and now all of a sudden she hates money. Nick Hades refuses to accept responsibility for robbing the American people. I blame him because his actions were responsible for creating such a huge, illegal fortune, and it is his actions that will continue to rob the American people. If Nora has divorced herself from this behavior, I welcome her change of heart. I want it known for the record that I have the least money of any senator in Congress. I am the only one who is not a millionaire. I am an actual outcast for being so poor."

"Our second question is from Bill and is directed to Senator Sandcastle."

"Thank you, Jim, and good evening, everyone. Senator, you have been an outspoken critic of President Hades' war policies. You have been quoted on the record as saying that you do not support sending more troops to Iraq, Syria, or Jordan. You are also on record as saying you do not support sending troops to South Korea or to Japan. You don't want to send troops to Afghanistan, to Yemen, to the Ukraine, or to Central America. Are you basically against our military way of life? Are you aware that if we stop deploying our forces, the U.S. economy will dive into a tailspin?"

"Bill, you need a good enema. Next question, please."

"Your response, Mr. President."

"Thank you, Bill. I want American citizens to know that a vote for Nick Hades is a vote for cruise missiles. You are voting for F-35s.

You are voting for new nuclear submarines. You are voting for supersonic drones. What would you rather have, these sleek new technological marvels or PBS?"

"Your response, Ms. Hades."

"I love the members of our armed forces. I just don't like the people who command them. As Commander In Chief, I will let all the other armies of the world fight and tear each other to pieces, while I keep our forces safe at home. Then we will beat the shit out of the winner."

"Now it's time for the second segment of our debate, questions from the audience. The first question is from Ms. Lacey McSnide of Appaloosa, Wisconsin."

"My question is for Nora Hades. Actually it isn't a question, it's a request. Could you please come out from behind the podium so we can see what you are wearing?"

# 69

"**G**ood morning to all.  I would like to thank members of the press for attending this news conference on such short notice.  My goodness, how did you guys ever get so many trucks and so many wires set up in a few hours?  As you can see, this podium is considerably larger than the one they gave me for the debates.

"Does everyone remember Ralph Nader?  He's the reason we had a war in Iraq.  Let me explain.  His candidacy enabled George W. Bush to beat Al Gore in Florida.  Gore lost by only 543 votes; Ralph Nader got 97,421.  If those votes had gone to Gore, he would easily have carried Florida, in spite of Republican Secretary of State Katherine Harris' dirty tricks.  Nationwide, Nader garnered 2,882,995 votes, or 2.74 percent of the popular vote.  There have been many presidential elections with slimmer margins than that.  In twenty-nine U.S. presidential contests, the margin of victory was less than 2,882,995.  John Kennedy beat Richard Nixon by just 112,827 votes.  Yes, his margin of victory was that small.  These are just historical election numbers, and you are wondering why I called this news conference.  As you all know, my poll numbers are very strong.  Senator Sandcastle's and President Hades' numbers are equally strong.

"I have some more numbers for you.  According to our system, the Electoral College, not the popular vote, elects the president. There are 538 electoral votes, and 270 are needed to win.  If the election results this November should mirror today's polls, each of us would wind up with 179 votes, plus or minus.  That's dividing 538 by three. In that case, none of us would be declared the winner. The president is then chosen by the House of Representatives, each state having just one vote. The candidate who wins a majority of votes, or twenty six states, becomes president. Nick Hades and his LiberTea Republicans hold an overwhelming majority in the House, and he would easily be declared the winner.

"I can't let that happen. I have asked another person to share the podium with me today. Before I go any further, I would like to have her join me here.

"Hello, Bernice."

"Hello, Nora."

"Bernice and I have been discussing the election. Neither of us will be selecting a vice-presidential candidate. We have decided to join forces. This does not mean that I'm abandoning the I. M. Wilde Party. On the contrary, most of our platform ideas will be incorporated into the co-platform we have developed, since Bernice and I are essentially in agreement on most issues. I will not become a Democrat but will remain a member of the Wilde Party. For the first time in U.S. History, the president and vice president will be from different parties. The United States of America desperately needs viable third-party and Independent candidates. Bernice Sandcastle is basically an Independent who caucuses with the Democrats. She won the Democratic nomination, but still has her Independent roots. I will let her explain how we intend to govern if we are lucky enough to be elected by the people."

"Thank you, Nora. We are going to have a shared presidency. By law, we can't both be president. We tossed a coin, and I won the

Presidency, so Nora will be vice president. However, she will not be a typical vice president. Those of us who know her know that she could never be typical at anything. It is my belief that the office of vice president has languished in inactivity and obscurity. In the past, *he* would just preside over the Senate, some ceremonial functions, and largely stay in the background while the president piloted the ship of state. But, if elected, *she* will do much more. We are elevating the office of vice president to that of co-president. I want to assure the American people that they are getting two fighters, not just one. There will be two chairs in the Oval Office. We will get twice as much done. We will not be intimidated by any Rethuglicans or Damnedocrats who put their own agenda ahead of this country.

"Here is the actual artwork for our campaign buttons, signs, and bumper stickers. They will be available in a few days. Doesn't Nora look good in red?"

"We will now take questions."

"Ms. Hades, has the president been told of your plans?"

# 70

"**G**ood morning, Euwee. You look like I feel. What on earth happened?"

"My wife and I got into a fight. She is not supporting your candidacy. We argued until four in the morning, and she threatened me with divorce."

I appreciate your loyalty, Euwee, but I do not want to hear any more bad news. My wife has joined the forces of light, and I cannot possibly win the election. She has done this deliberately to spite me. Actually, she probably was not thinking about me at all. She has an unquenchable thirst for center stage. She is now guaranteed top media exposure for another eight years, instead of just four more years. I can see her next shopping trip, picking out new colors of sequined knickers. I am telling you, Euwee, she is a couple of sandwiches short of a picnic. Between Nora and Bernice, they are going to need seven shrinks on their cabinet to keep them functioning in a straight line. Their cabinet will have more than a few screws loose. What else do you have for me?"

"Mr. President, the chef you hired....."

"And that Nora fired. The sadistic bitch!"

"Yes, Mr. President, Fifi LaFlamme...."

"What about Fifi LaFlamme?"

"I have a top-secret file here from the CIA. Fifi's real name is Olga Rodchenko, and she is a KGB operative."

"No wonder the woman could not cook worth a shit! But then, I did not hire her for her buns, at least not those made of flour. I did not notice any Russian accent. No harm was done, was there?"

"Well sir, there is a photograph in today's *Washington Post* of you and Ms. Rodchenko together in your fold-out Oval Office bed, with the caption. 'Hades Betrays the U.S. in Love Tryst with Russian Spy.' It seems she successfully hacked into White House and Pentagon security systems from your computer, and transmitted the names of all our agents, who are posing as transvestite stock brokers, back to Russia. Someone high up leaked the story to the paper."

"Is that all?"

"No, there's more, Mr. President. Percy Floy was arrested in Iowa."

"Who the hell cares? He is dead to me."

"Mr. President there is a complication. It seems that the former vice president bought thousands of acres of fertile farmland and planted a marijuana crop. The Iowa legislature, backed by all the state's religious groups, defeated the amendment to make the crop legal in Iowa. Since possession is against the law, he is being prosecuted for intent to distribute."

"I repeat, who the hell cares? That is his problem."

"Sir, he has made you co-owner of the business, and your name is on the land deeds. Your name is also listed as half-owner of the property where the silos full of the illegal crop are stored. Naturally it has all been confiscated. The federal court in Iowa is preparing to take legal action against you, sir. I believe Floy's motive is revenge."

"Is there any other news this morning, Euwee?"

"Yes sir, there is more."

"Oh goody, I cannot fucking wait to hear it."

"As you know, there is a World Summit meeting in Brussels in two weeks. All the heads of state of Europe and Asia are planning to address world trade, global warming, and military cooperation. You were not invited, sir."

"Fuck 'em. What else have you got?"

"The three major networks, most cable news services, and PBS all refuse to broadcast your next Fireside Chat."

"Damn it, Euwee! It is not a Fireside Chat. I call it Significations and Redemptions. We say a prayer and sing 'God Bless America.' What more do they want?"

"You can call it a Chat From Your Fairy Godfather for all I care, sir. I quit! I can no longer stand the stress, or the hypocrisy. You will have to find yourself another chief of staff."

# 71

"It is three a.m., and I am sitting in the Oval Office. I made my own peanut butter and jelly sandwiches, and mixed my own spiked apple cider. Actually, I like mine better than Madeleine's because I pour in much more bourbon. I am doing things differently, and am not writing anything down. Instead of verbalizing my ideas and then putting ink on paper, I am using a miniature digital recorder. By speaking directly, without the cumbersome waiting and pausing that writing causes, my ideas are fast, furious, and immediate, no stoppages. I will transcribe everything later, since I know it will someday be of tremendous historical importance to all Americans. The Nick Hades Library in Indiana will probably play this tape long after I am gone, as the ultimate example of human resolve and determination.

"If anyone thinks I am going to just fade away quietly with my tail between my legs, they have made a grievous miscalculation. As John Paul Smith once said, 'I have not yet begun to begin.' This is not my fight to lose, it is their fight to win, and I am not fighting to lose, so they cannot win. It really is so simple. When you corner a Komodo Dragon, you have more than a tiger by the tail. You have a fierce creature who fears nothing. I asked a simple question of America. It was the same question asked by another great president. I asked not what your country could do for you, I asked what you could do for me. Instead of telling me what you could do *for* me, you told me what you are going to do *to* me. So now in this political retrospective, I must reevaluate my relationship with my family and the American sheeple.

"Nora is nuts, but she still puts out. Kinky sex is good sex. Therefore, for now at least, we should stay together. Alfonso is all boy. Someday he will make a great general. He will be a great drone controller, while his sister Petunia will join her mother and drone on all day long about I. M. Wilde. There is no way I will let Bernice Sandcastle and Nora sit at this desk while I slink quietly away into the night in disgrace.

"Jboo, Itch, and Helena Handbasket are ready to implement my plans. First thing in the morning, we go to a Code Red Terrorist Alert. My friend Ralphie in the CIA will blow up a few buildings, hopefully without killing too many sheeple. Sometimes I have to sacrifice a few to safeguard my American way of life. I will present evidence that this attack originated in the UAP (Unified Arab Protectorates) and was ordered by Grand Sultan Prince Demented himself. This will allow me to start a limited war, and pay that towelhead back for speaking in front of the U.S. Congress without my permission.

"Do not forget for one minute that I am Commander in Chief. When our military is happy, and they are always happiest when they kill foreigners – and some domestics, but mostly foreigners – then that happiness trickles down to Joe and Jane Sheeple. As always, my poll numbers will rise. Since the stakes will be much higher, so will be my ratings.

"I will place my family, including Nora, or rather especially Nora, into protective custody in a remote, closely guarded bunker north of Camp David. I do not want them to be targeted by agents of the UAP. Naturally, in a private conversation with my lovely wife, I will offer to remove the protective custody if she agrees not to run as President of Vice.

"Bart Bassa will supervise drone flybys over Sandcastle's house. We intend to do this at all hours of the day and night. We will remove all mufflers from the drone engines. We will claim this is necessary to safeguard an important presidential candidate, but the real purpose is to break down her senses and drive her crazy.

"Percy Flyweight Floy will fail miserably to have me indicted in his pot party. I will claim executive immunity to all civilian laws because the nation is having a military crisis. I will make sure he is in jail, however, so he can cause no more trouble.

"Well, that should about cover it. Nora and Sandcastle will be out of the way, the election will be postponed until further notice, and my ratings will rise dramatically."

"Mr. President."

"Yes, who is speaking please?"

"This is Sergeant Major Yorp of White House Security, and I'm at the front desk, sir."

"What can I do for you, Sergeant Major?"

"There are some people here who want to talk to you. Should I send them up, sir?"

"Who are they?"

"Percy Floy, Itch McCringle, Jboo Boehnhead, Helena Handbasket, Nora Hades, Petunia Hades, Alfonso Hades, Bernice Sandcastle, Samantha Sandcastle, Karl Krotch, Adolph Krotch,

Dwayne Lapoopierre, Clarabell Thomas, Rhoda Dendron, Sarah Lapin, Ludwig Peckeroff, Coin Goldman, Antibody Scalia, Sameold Alito, Harvey Schwartz, Jim McCann, Daniel Grouse, Dirk Groggin, Vladimir Putin, Ludmila Kasyanenko, Natalia Bulgakov, Olga Rodchenko, Fanny Mucha, Foxxy Hart, Myra Glock, Sal DiPalma, Madeleine Soufflé, Reverend Normal Nabertwackle, Flossie Filbert, Joe Liberstraum, Joe the Jackhammer, Betty Median, Ms. Lacey McSnide, Howard Howitzer, Mrs. Essy Tool, Nomad Tool, Lucy, Alice, Clara, Agent Crawdad, Mary Ellen Nonsense, Junco Inman, Dribble J. Lesser, Crug Picknose, Bart Bassa, Sultan Prince Demented, Gnarly Schaefer, Pariah Winfredo, Michelle Bacchanalia, Ann Cutlet, Carla Gung, Jan McDrewer, Jim Trapezoid, Hymie Wart, Bill O'Hara, Jennifer, Ralph, Euwee Crinkle, Frau Hymnler, and Snotty Droopy Dingo Doggy.

"The Oval Office is kind of small for sixty-five people. Should I send them up to the main conference room, sir?

"Sir?"

Joe Randazzo is the author of nine previous books, including six novels and *Going With the Wind*, a photo-documentary on North and South Carolina. His artwork has been exhibited at many venues throughout New England, including Castleton State College, T. W. Wood Art Gallery, and the Helen Day Art Center. He lives with his wife Rita in South Burlington, Vermont.

www.ingramcontent.com/pod-product-compliance
Lightning Source LLC
Chambersburg PA
CBHW031827090426
42741CB00005B/154